A Way with Animals

*The question is not, Can they reason?
nor, Can they talk? but, Can they suffer?*

—JEREMY BENTHAM: The Principles of
 Morals and Legislation,
 XVII, *1789*

A Studio Book
The Viking Press, New York

A Way with Animals

Bruce Buchenholz

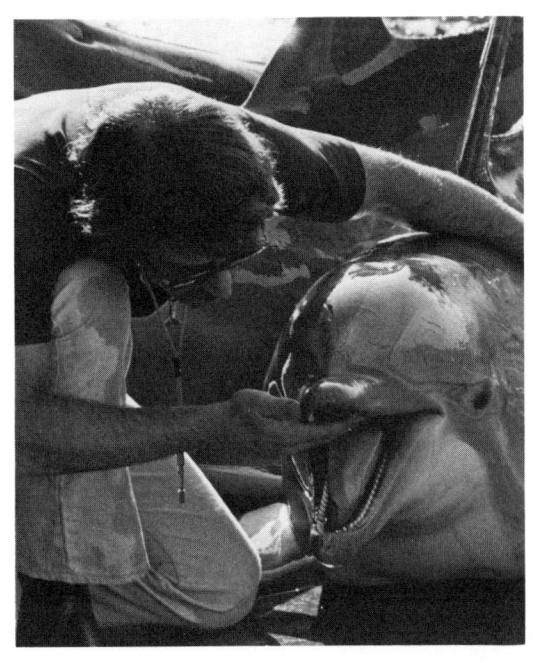

Dedication

The old mutt was a bag of skin and bones. He didn't see very well. He didn't hear very well. He didn't eat very well. He'd been very close to us for many years, but as he gradually withdrew he acquired a kind of independence that was somehow primeval and majestic.

He didn't object to us, not even to our handling. He was just passive and detached. He paced constantly in a steady long-distance trot from one end of the house to the other. Day after day. When his pacing brought him to a corner he just stood there until someone backed him out. It wasn't so much that he couldn't see. He just couldn't go backward; his drive was onward. And when spoken to it wasn't so much that he couldn't hear; he was listening to a different voice. It was calling him.

A monotonous, rhythmical, pulsating dance of death, an inexorably beating pavane to the call of the unknown. He had left the pack and was off into the forest, mile after mile after mile.

He had a life of love and a death of great majesty.

Yet there are secret moments when I still hear his voice.

The behavior of men to the lower animals, and their behavior to each other, bear a constant relationship.

—HERBERT SPENCER: Social Statics, IV, *1851*

Copyright © Bruce Buchenholz, 1978
All rights reserved
First published in 1978 by The Viking Press
625 Madison Avenue, New York, N.Y. 10022
Published simultaneously in Canada by
Penguin Books Canada Limited

Library of Congress Cataloging in Publication Data
Buchenholz, Bruce.
  A way with animals.
  (A Studio book)
  1. Animals, Training of. 2. Animals, Habits and Behavior of. I. Title.
GV1829.B83   636.08'8   77-27656
ISBN 0-670-75256-8

Printed in the United States of America

Contents

Preface 6
Deep Down Devotion 9
Love Is Not Enough 31
Cerberus 43
Old Gray Mares Need Not Apply 57
The Norman Conquest 71
Behold Now Behemoth 87
Mayhem in High Places 103
One Great Ape 123
Afterword 143

Preface

On the street where I live there used to be a man with a Doberman. They were a phenomenal pair. I have never seen a dog so perfectly trained in the image of his "master" (the word is most apt). The man, in his late thirties, had sparse blond hair, an erect bearing, and a pale, chilly, expressionless face. He walked stiffly, rapidly, and straight, head up and eyes front. The dog too had a cold, expressionless face. He walked at a perfect heel, stiffly, rapidly, and erect, head up and eyes front. The man spoke to no one, greeted no neighbors, strode down the street like a Teutonic god. The dog was utterly oblivious to other animals and people. They made such an effect that anyone in their path would automatically step out of their way, as if to avoid being mowed down.

The first time my mastiff puppy saw them at some distance he started the rump-wagging little bounds that meant he was working himself up to greet a new dog. By the time the pair came abreast of us my puppy was in full action, panting, bounding about, leaping toward the Doberman, inviting him to play, and being as provocative as he could be. An excited mastiff puppy, even then as large as the Doberman, is not a presence easily ignored. But that pair strode by without the slightest break in their style, without the flicker of an eyelash, without any indication that the street wasn't completely deserted. The puppy came to a dazed halt, stared briefly at the stiff departing backs, and turned his attention to a leaf blown by a breeze.

That experience made a big impression on me. I started wondering about people and their animals. I wondered if, in general, people related to animals the same ways they relate to each other. Is it the same game of the "self" and the "other" that we're playing all the time? With animals, as with people, do we start by creating a make-believe barrier and then proceed to strengthen or weaken it, attack it or defend it, reshape it? Is our relationship with animals the same dance around "the wall between" that we perform with each other?

As a consequence of writing and photographing over the years I have had somewhat more than average lay experience with animals. In the course of a medical practice of psychiatry and psychoanalysis for even more years I have had a lot of experience with people. I decided that this experience at least provided a position from which I could better define some of the questions in my mind.

It seemed best to acquaint myself with a varied sample of working relationships between people and animals. I would first talk to the people in an unstructured way and take note of what evolved from the conversation. I would watch them interact with their animals to see what I could see. I would photograph with equal spontaneity and explore what the pictures disclosed.

One could hardly devise a more subjective technique for the avowed purpose of seeking information! That, in fact, is one of the chief things I learned from the whole procedure. I learned that questions which have validity and vitality for me might seem totally irrelevant to you. Any answers I might dream up could be judged only on aesthetic grounds, as creative acts.

I shall not, therefore, foist my questions and answers on you in a heavy-handed way. I'll just invite you to share the experiences, the conversations, the pictures. You can consider my own reactions, when you notice them, as just another aspect of the experience. Then you can find questions and answers that are personal to you.

BRUCE BUCHENHOLZ
April 1977

P.S. If you don't like questions and answers, come along just for fun.

Deep Down Devotion

Who hears the fishes when they cry?
—Thoreau: A Week on the Concord
and Merrimack Rivers, *1849*

Nobody knows Arnie like Jim Mullen does, so I'm going to let him tell you about Arnie in his own words:

When you're working in a show with a team of dolphins and the leader is a sulky animal, man, you're in trouble! This dolphin Arnie, he's been around a long time and he's worked with lots of trainers. He knows the whole setup. The other two male dolphins, they're just his muscle-men, his "go-fers." They carry out the orders. If Arnie gets p-o'ed at one of the animals, doesn't like the way he did something, that animal gets nudged out of line in the next behavior. You're standing on the stage expecting four dolphins to go leaping over the hurdle in line. Three of 'em arch over in perfect symmetry and there's no sign of the other one—like he just disappeared. He didn't disappear. They just put the fear of God into him and he's afraid to show his face. If Arnie is in a bad mood on a particular day, he can mess up the entire show. He usually doesn't do anything wrong himself but he gives the orders. I can see him look at them. I see the eye contact.

I'm supposed to be the trainer, the one who decides what they're going to do, the one whose cues they follow. Arnie doesn't always see it that way. Then it's a challenge for control of the group. It's mind against mind. And sometimes Arnie wins. He's got very strong willpower.

One time there was a part of the show he'd been doing perfectly for a year and then it suddenly got sloppy. He just got careless about it. I insisted it should go right. Didn't work. I tried again. Didn't work. He had just decided that he wanted to do it half-assed. The next show he didn't even bother to come over to the station. He was showing me that he'd decided he didn't want to do *anything*. I stood there on the platform and looked at the audience and I looked at the three dolphins neatly lined up at the station in front of me and I said to Arnie, "Who needs ya? I got these others who can do it."

So there were these animals out there trying to work and there was Arnie swimming around and around them making them nervous. Then we got to the tail walk, where they get up vertically on their tails and sort of walk backwards on the surface of the water. The three of them got up neatly in line and Arnie swept along the line knocking each one over like a bowling pin. I got them up again. Down they went again. I got through that show only because the audience thought it was part of the act and they loved it.

I wasn't looking forward to the next show later that day. Sure enough, Arnie stayed off to the side. You know what I did? I ignored the audience. *I* went over to *him* and started to talk to him in a low voice. It was kind of stupid. I hadn't fed him for two days since he started this hassle. I showed him a fish and I asked very nicely for him to come get it. No way. So I threw him the fish. You know what the creep did? He caught the fish and spit it out. He was hungry but he *spat it out!*

I got another fish, held it out, and this time he came over. I wasn't fooled. I knew he came for the satisfaction of spitting it back at me again. But instead of giving him the fish, what I did was pet him. I didn't say I was sorry but I was thinking that he really had all the cards stacked against him and I had to admire his guts, and I petted him. After a moment of what must have been shock, his head perked up. Then I offered him the fish and he swallowed it in kind of a dazed way.

From that point on I praised that animal lavishly for every little thing he did. And from that point on he worked. I could get him out of a bad mood every time. Well, he's sensitive and he's stubborn, so it's not *every* time, but *almost* every time. I had a kid here working with me and he said, "If I didn't see it with my own eyes I wouldn't believe it." I said, "Me neither." That Arnie is some creepy dolphin!

Jim Mullen and his dolphins work at Marine World–Africa USA in Redwood City, California. I spent many hours watching them work and saw a great many noteworthy things, but the one overriding impression I got was of the respect they had for each other. I felt very strongly that both animals and man were fully justified in that respect. Jim's feelings about dolphins were apparent in what he told me about their training:

We get these animals from the ocean. These are bottlenose dolphins, Atlantic or Pacific,

This is Jim and three-quarters of his team. (Arnie was sent away because he refused to smile for the picture.)

and they're used to rather shallow water. So the pools are no great problem for them. But you have to stop and think of what's involved in the transition from ocean to man-made environment. Generally, most cetacean species seem not to be very aggressive. They don't seem to have the same natural fear of man that other animals do. You hear so many stories of dolphins saving humans at sea, pushing them to shore. But maybe they push some guys *away* from the shore; the guys wouldn't be around to tell those stories. Dolphins just seem to push things around. They'll push a dead baby dolphin around for days. You might say that's not a very intelligent thing for a supposedly intelligent animal to do. But who knows? Maybe it's an emotional thing. We don't really understand that much about dolphins in the ocean because the dolphins we know, those who live with us, are a whole other thing. To grasp that, you have to picture the freedom, and especially the openness, of their life in the ocean.

Then the dolphin gets captured, transported and stuck in a tank. Every detail of his life and surroundings is controlled by man, a creature he's likely never to have seen before. Just think of what his sonar system has to go through and his digestive system, which suddenly has to deal with dead fish. To say nothing of his nervous system and the emotional shocks. That process of acclimation is a prolonged, tortured birth process. And the

This is a tail walk. The dolphins are about to walk backward on the surface of the water.

animal who emerges is a new creature, a humanized dolphin.

That new dolphin is very sensitive. He's going to emerge from the acclimation and training process deeply marked by the man responsible for him. You can tell a man by his dog, but you can even more easily tell the basic personality of the fellow who worked with this dolphin. Things you wouldn't even notice about yourself, little things, subtleties, that dolphin notices very keenly and reacts to sharply. You could, for instance, get a little aggravated about something. Being a nice, calm, gentle guy, maybe you'd stamp your foot a little, make a face, and forget the whole thing. But that dolphin in the tank has his attention riveted on you and that little foot stamp goes through his nervous system like an earthquake. The first four to six months of captivity shape the animal's personality. He

Arnie likes to do this flip; it gives him a chance to splash people.

brings from the ocean whatever potential he has and with that he adapts to captivity and develops his "captive personality."

Naturally, when you meet a new dolphin, a naïve animal, you have to expect he'll be pretty apprehensive. Sometimes you're lucky if he stays still long enough to eat. You have to throw the food to him while he's dashing around in circles. Nowadays you usually get animals from a middleman who has acclimated them and guarantees you a "feeder." The animal has had a little experience with glass, concrete, strange noises, and strange diet, but now he's got one more person to adjust to and one more move. If you just move an animal across the street, it'll take him seven to ten days to get over the experience.

After the show, everybody comes for the critique.

Well, here you have this new life, this new creature you're responsible for, and there's a barrier that has to be broken down. You have to establish a rapport. It's like making a new friend. You have to be aware of what he's up against and you feed him carefully and talk nicely and move gently. You build up a friendship.

While you're doing that you accustom him to a "bridging stimulus." That's a sound you make with a dog whistle, a police whistle, an underwater sound system, whatever you like. From now on that sound will be his cue. Pretty soon he associates that sound with food and you've got yourself going. You're ready to teach him a behavior.

Cetaceans are not like dogs and horses. The fact is that once you've helped them acclimate and established a good relationship, you've already done the tricky part of the job.

Sometimes a private conference is necessary in order to avoid embarrassing a team member.

Teaching them behaviors is easy because you don't have to get the idea more than half across and they'll meet you the other half. You have to show a dog over and over again what you want him to do. Not so the dolphin. You start showing them something and they'll pick it up and take it the rest of the way. And then they'll innovate, and if you're wise you'll consider seriously any suggestion they make. These animals are smart, which is why there are a hell of a lot of people so successful in this business today. I don't mind saying that. We all get a star syndrome. I went through that too, just like everybody else. You get out there, make signals, the animals do these great things, and the people clap for you and think you're terrific. And I guess it's natural; you want to believe them.

When you start teaching a dolphin behaviors, it's best to start with something simple, natural, and unstressful. Just expand some natural behavior, like jumping. They jump, you whistle and give them food. You do that a couple of times and the animal figures he's got you trained—that he can make you give him a fish every time he gives you the jump signal. So you have to use what we call an "interrupted schedule of reinforcement." You don't feed the animal every time he does something. You get him to try it again, and maybe again. You teach him to keep trying until you're satisfied that he's doing it just right. He mustn't expect to get fed every time he does a certain thing, because if he sets the standards, he's going to sulk if you don't do everything just the way he expects.

You can get a dolphin ready for a complete show in six months. It could take longer, but not because the animal isn't intelligent. I've never yet met a dumbbell. A fellow I was working with insisted he had a dumb dolphin. I said that couldn't be and insisted he was doing something wrong. He said that not only was he doing nothing wrong but that he had tried more things than I ever knew existed. Anyhow, it turned out that his dolphin had a tumor. We were both right: the dolphin wasn't dumb and the trainer wasn't doing anything wrong.

So why does it take a little or a lot longer to train one dolphin than another? Because they have such different personalities—as dif-

ferent as day and night. Each one is an individual and each of these individuals has had a different experience during those first few months of captivity. That's why I treat them as individuals. Some fellows deal with their show animals as a team. If one of the animals does something wrong, nobody gets fed. The trainer figures that this way the others will get on the wrongdoer and yank him back in line. It often works, too, but I figure that the wrongdoer is my problem and that anybody who does his behavior right is entitled to eat. I want each individual to know that as long as he does his thing right he'll get fed even if the others mess up the act. That's not always so easy, because even if one of them wants to do right he may be afraid to go against the group. And sometimes you have to think fast, because tricky decisions have to be made on the spur of the moment.

The other day Arnie made a pass at the female just as the show was about to start. She turned him down and he whacked her. She stayed out of the first behavior. Well, do I give Arnie a fish? He did the first behavior fine, but he made her stay out. On the spot, I

decided to give Arnie a fish and not to give her one. You see, it was a performance and he performed and she didn't. He may have been the cause of her failure, but she's responsible for her performance. I gave Arnie the fish because he performed, and I probably shouldn't get involved with their private lives anyway. Arnie is very sensitive to things like acceptance or rejection.

I don't know if I made the right decision or if I made a mistake. I make mistakes. The trick is not to make the same mistakes over and over again. These animals are very sharp and you have to make sure that sharpness is working for you and not against you. For example, many trainers have certain mannerisms, gestures, habits unconsciously associated with their activities. So, quite unaware, they telegraph what they're about to do. If, for example, you're thinking to give them the signal to applaud, to clap their flippers, you might unconsciously move your elbows out just a fraction. If you do that with any consistency, you're going to end up with dolphins who'll go through a whole act while you're thinking about it. You have to see it once to understand it. You get ready to have them do a certain thing, you look up, and they're halfway through it. If you don't realize what's going on, you get a very weird feeling. There's a trainer in Australia who just published an article about how he communicates with his dolphins by telepathy. He says he's got this system where all he has to do is think which behavior he wants them to do and they do it. He was cited by Queen Juliana of the Netherlands. I expect that if I watched him I could see what was really going on. I haven't seen, so I don't know, but I'd have to admit that it's my suspicion that if those dolphins couldn't see him they couldn't read his mind.

19

These animals think. They're always figuring. You have to keep them from outsmarting themselves. If anybody anticipates me, I'll call him back in. He's wrong. And he immediately knows he's wrong and why. I always exercise them with a variety of deliberately misleading signals. They get rewarded only for responding at the right time to the right cues.

That's the story Jim told me, and I felt I had learned a great deal about working with animals, about dolphins, and about Jim. Then I spent a lot of time watching all these things. After a while I would recognize what Jim was doing and why he was doing it, what he was after. Then I'd be pleased with myself and think that I was being pretty smart. When I realized that the dolphins were catching on, too, I was a little deflated. When I further realized that they often grasped it *faster* than I did, I quickly told myself that fish is my least favorite food anyhow.

Jim came over and sat next to me on the lowest tier of the benches overlooking the pool. It was a clear, crisp day and the sun was burning down on us, making the water sparkle and making us feel like just lolling around. The dolphins were looping about in circles and they too seemed to be taking it easy. Across from us, at the opposite end of the oval pool, a diver in a wet suit was adjusting some equipment. Time seemed to be jogging in place. Jim, leaning on his elbow, said, "They're restless." I asked what he meant. He said, "They're acting this way because I'm

This is the head of a killer whale. If you can find his eye, you will see that he is looking at you suspiciously.

hanging around. They can't figure out what I'm doing. Usually when I'm here I'm actively engaged with them. And the female there, she's bored."

I told him that if he was going to talk like that he'd better show more respect for the Australian trainer with his telepathy. "Oh no," said Jim. "Just as they get to understand my habitual moves and reactions, I get to understand theirs. Besides, she's telling me she's bored."

By this time I had heard and seen too much to be incredulous about anything that Jim said about what goes on between himself and the dolphins. I just asked, "What do you mean?"

"Listen carefully next time she comes by," Jim said. I did so, but despite the stillness of the air that seemed to magnify all sounds, I heard only the lapping of the water, the cries of the ever-present gulls, and, as if at a great distance, small equipment sounds from the diver across the pool. Jim encouraged me to keep listening, and, sure enough, during the female's next pass I heard faint, high-pitched clicking sounds like those made by a Geiger counter.

"That's it," Jim said. "She's impatient for the diver to get in the water. He'll be a diversion but, even more important, he'll drop things, weights or tools, and she'll then have something to play with."

As we sat around the pool that lazy afternoon Jim told me how he initially got involved with aquatic mammals:

You know, I'm only the assistant training director. If you want to learn something you should spend some time with Sonny Allen. He's the Director of Training. He taught me, and he got me my first job. We were kids in Philadelphia and we had a singing group. We were pretty good, too. Did some records, played the Catskill circuit, Grossinger's, the works. But we all did other things too. I trained dogs. Sonny was a diver. We hung around on a street corner in South Philly and right across the street they were building the

new aquarium. I went into military service and when I got back the aquarium was finished and Sonny was working there. He got me a job there as fish-room cutter and feeder. I fed the birds. They'd flutter and fuss around out there and I'd throw the food at them. After a while it got my goat that they stayed way the hell off in the distance and made me throw all that stuff. I felt that if they wanted the food they could damn well come to me. So eventually they came. Then I started to use the food as a lure, to get them to do things. I could get them to follow me or to climb up shallow stairs. Just the simplest things, but these were pelicans and penguins and to get them to do *anything* is amazing. Man, those birds are stupid!

After a while I graduated to doing a clown dive in the show. I'd climb up on this thirty-foot-high board, clown around, fall in the water, and the dolphins would save me. I'd never seen a dolphin before. And I'd never been in the water with anything bigger than a sand crab. When you realize that the sand crab scared me, you'll have some idea of how I felt being in the water with those seven-foot gray hulks sliding by. I was deathly afraid. But after a while the fear went away and as strong as the fear had been, that's how strong my liking for it developed.

Then I got with the pilot whales. I didn't know anything about pilot whales and I didn't know anything about training, so I did a very smart thing—I did exactly what Sonny told me to do and only what Sonny told me to do. And that's all I did until Sonny got this job out here and sent for me. That was almost ten years ago and I've learned a lot on my own, but Sonny was the one who taught me enough so I *could* learn on my own.

So I talked with Sonny Allen. He, too, proudly told me about the singing group. His initial job with Aquarama in Philadelphia was as a diver. He had been diving since he was twelve years old, so he had much more of a water background than Jimmy did. From the beginning of his work in Philadelphia he'd been interested in the training and spent a lot of time watching the trainers, and after a couple of years they let him do some work with pilot whales. Sonny then studied behavioral psychology at the University of Pennsylvania and eventually became director of training at Aquarama. He was there for more than seven years until they went into bankruptcy. Some of the animals from Aquarama went to Marine World–Africa USA and Sonny went with them. At Marine World's request he agreed to help them get set up. He planned to stay there six months and then go back to school. But the six months have stretched into nine years now and Sonny is running the show. Since Jim was so respectful of Sonny's knowledge and ability, I asked Sonny about the killer whales he's currently working with. He said:

When we first brought the killer whales in from British Columbia I knew absolutely nothing about them. I hired Herb Reid, who was experienced with them, and he taught me whatever I know about killer whales. The first thing that comes to my mind is that the killer whale has no fear of anything. He is afraid of absolutely nothing. This has a number of significant consequences. It's easiest to see if you compare them with dolphins. You get a dolphin in from the ocean and you have to fuss with him for month after month. You have to approach him slowly, coax and cajole him, ease him into everything. The killer whale from the ocean has the same big adjustment to make, but he doesn't have to get over being afraid of anything—because he's *not* afraid. He could be acclimated in as little as three weeks. We had one killer whale right out of the ocean and three months later he had eighteen behaviors and was ready to go to work.

Probably on the same account they learn three times faster than the dolphin. That's because two-thirds of the time necessary to teach a dolphin a new behavior isn't spent in teaching him, it's spent in getting him to accept the new situation. If, for example, you want to get him to jump over a hurdle, you have to go through a lot of "approximations" to get him used to the hurdle first. With a dolphin you have to jolly him along and convince him that it's okay—*then* he learns quickly.

A killer whale, on the other hand, doesn't have such problems. You put a hurdle, or for that matter anything else, in the water and a killer whale won't even flinch. When I first saw their incredible learning capacity, it completely blew me out. You put a hurdle in the water with a killer whale and he's not going to act like you might be threatening to disrupt his universe. He's going to take it in stride, and by the next session you'll have him going over it.

It's so easy that you tend to forget what you're working with. You have to keep in mind at all times with these animals that their name must mean *something*. You can only push them so far—one step further and they'll get belligerent. You could get bitten and that could be very bad. These animals are never to be considered fully domesticated. When the head starts to tremble, the eyes get big and red, the tail slaps—watch out. That means you've upset him. You've done something wrong and you'd better cool everything until you figure out what it is. It's always your responsibility. If that animal gets miffed, it means you did something wrong. If you can't take the blame and if that animal has to suffer on your account, you shouldn't be around animals. You had better remember that without the animal you wouldn't even be a trainer.

That's the thing. You can't have a dominating attitude. You have to be reasonable and work in harmony with the animal. For that you have to understand each individual. Just as with a human being, you could destroy an animal mentally and physically by playing with his emotions. We try to train these animals in the most relaxed atmosphere possible. If they're in a bad mood, we don't work them. If *we're* in a bad mood, we don't work them. They know your mood and your attitude. The moment you hit the stage they know the whole score—even if you don't. My rule for my staff is that if you have a personal problem or a bad mood or a cold, don't go near the animals. If, on the other hand, you're relaxed, the chances are the animals will be relaxed and the chances are you'll be able to make clear split-second decisions.

The whole thing gets down to awareness. You have to know how the animal feels, and why. And you have to know how you feel, and why. You have to give it all you've got. I channel all my energies to the animal I'm working with. Of course, I get attached to the animals—very much so. The closer the relationship, the better off you are. If you're not open, if you put up a closed, defensive emotional barrier, that limits how far you'll be able to go with that animal.

You might as well be open. He's going to pick up your feelings anyhow. Hell, the animal even picks up the personality traits of his trainer. Like Jimmy, for example. Jimmy Mullen's dolphins are slow, easygoing, good-natured.

I've heard a number of very experienced people say that the animal (dog, elephant, dolphin, whale, etc.) picks up the personality traits of its owner, trainer, handler. They each claimed they could observe an animal and tell a lot about its trainer. When asked about the traits of their *own* animals, however, they seemed to dissociate. Each would talk about his animal as an individual and would be inarticulate about traits he himself might have in common with his animals. It was always the *other* fellow they could read like a book through his animals.

I told Jimmy Mullen what Sonny had said about his dolphins. Mullen replied, "Well, if that's what Sonny said, I guess that's the way it is. It's true, I'm not an aggressive person. But you take my dolphin Arnie, for example. The other day he was doing a high-jump. I held up high this very long pole with a fish on its tip, and he jumped up and grabbed the fish. But this time he missed the fish and took a bite of the pole. He must have been disappointed or frustrated, because he took that very badly. When they all lined up to wave good-bye to the audience, he came back to the stage with the others but he didn't wave. You could tell he was p-o'ed. The dolphins were waving and the audience was clapping and you know what he did? He jumped up on the platform and walloped me! Nearly knocked me into the water. He blamed *me* that he didn't get that fish. I can't see his reasoning in that, because he was the guy doing the jumping. Maybe he figured I held the pole wrong. I guess so. That Arnie, he's some creepy dolphin!"

Love Is Not Enough

Nature is not lavish of her beauties.
—Byron: *Letter to John Murray,
February 7, 1821*

Shimon the Bedouin camel trainer tells this story:

"This was in the winter when the camels want to come to their wives. At this time they are very dangerous—they bite. They only look for woman. I climb on the camel. After five kilometers the camel starts to be nervous. He starts to run back to his wife seventy kilometers an hour and he eats the ropes. I cannot get off because he eats the ropes. When he comes to his wife I kick him very hard and he bites my leg so that I bleed very much and have big scar even now. The camel goes on his wife and I am on the camel. From this I have trouble with my back."

The thousands of years of relationship between man and the camel have resulted in what can best be described as an uneasy armed truce. The camel does what's required of him —most of the time—and the Bedouin takes care of the camel—most of the time. Neither gets romantic or sentimental about the other.

"Every morning you need to give him mixed flour and oil. Olive oil. You mix it, you put it in a big spoon and you give him. Once my grandmother was to go to the market and get this and take care of the camel. But she didn't get it so he get her and break her."

The training of a camel usually starts when the animal is about three years old. The keys to the process are a small hole cut in the camel's nose when he is quite young—the "rope hole"—and the fact that in summer the camel needs more food and water than in winter. The camel is left outside the tent for five days without food. The trainer then approaches and tries to lead him with a rope tied through the rope hole. If the camel refuses, the process is repeated five days later. After no more than twenty days of starvation the camel will usually allow himself to be led. He is given a little food and the trainer walks with him around and around a small area. The camel is then taught to sit on command. The order is spoken (in the Negev desert the sound is something like a guttural "Chhhr") and the camel is tapped with a stick behind his front knees at the same time as the nose rope is pulled down. When the camel sits he is again rewarded with food. It usually requires several days to teach this command.

In the next phase of training, the trainer climbs on the camel (always from the left side) and allows him to get accustomed to a man on his back. At this stage two ropes are attached to the nose hole, one held by the rider on the right side of the camel's neck, the other on the left. When the animal has become accustomed to carrying the trainer, the ropes are used to pull his head in the direction the rider wishes to go. As he pulls the rope on one side, the trainer taps the camel with a stick on the opposite side. When the camel has learned this well, the right-hand rope is removed, the left is allowed to go slack, and the signal is given only with the stick. The remaining rope on the left side is thereafter used chiefly to control the camel from the ground. To increase

the camel's pace, the stick is used, along with a verbal command ("Hite!"). The nose rope is pulled and the command "Gif" is given to get the camel to stop. In about two months the camel learns to be led, to kneel, to accept a rider, to rise (again "Hite!" or a cluck as when urging a horse forward), to move forward and to the side, and to stop. During this time the camel is rewarded with increasing quantities of food until his normal intake is reached. After about three months the camel has learned these commands well enough to be worked.

Since the camel is primarily a beast of

The relationship is that of an uneasy armed truce. The camel does what's required—most of the time.

burden, this basic training usually suffices. The animal can then carry men or commodities. After the camel is fully matured (about five years) he can carry up to three hundred kilograms (about six hundred sixty pounds), although it is thought that to do so consistently would shorten his work life. The camel lives from thirty to fifty years. I was told that the life span is influenced by adequacy and regularity of feeding, regulation of the work load, and limitation of sexual activity.

Camels are domesticated animals (although there are a few scattered wild herds such as the one in Spain) and are, therefore, completely dependent on humans. In certain situations, as, for example, on the Sahara, the dependency is mutual. It is apparent from folklore that the camel is respected for his strength, his keen hearing, and even for his independence and sexual prowess. But there is no indication of any general fondness for the creature, and there are only rare instances of a Bedouin-camel pair with a bond of affection. One Bedouin told me that his camel liked him, and he knew this because the camel worked hard without urging and always won races for him. He claimed that at one time, during the rutting season, the camel left a group of females and came running for him. He escaped but was so frightened that he decided to sell the camel, only to realize that he couldn't bear to part with it.

Camels are used to transport people, to pull, to haul, and to provide sport (e.g., camel races and camel fights). In a few areas camels are put to military use; the Trucial Oman Scouts use them on the Arabian desert, and the Israeli Army Camel Patrol on the Sinai desert. The Israeli Patrol is essentially an intelli-

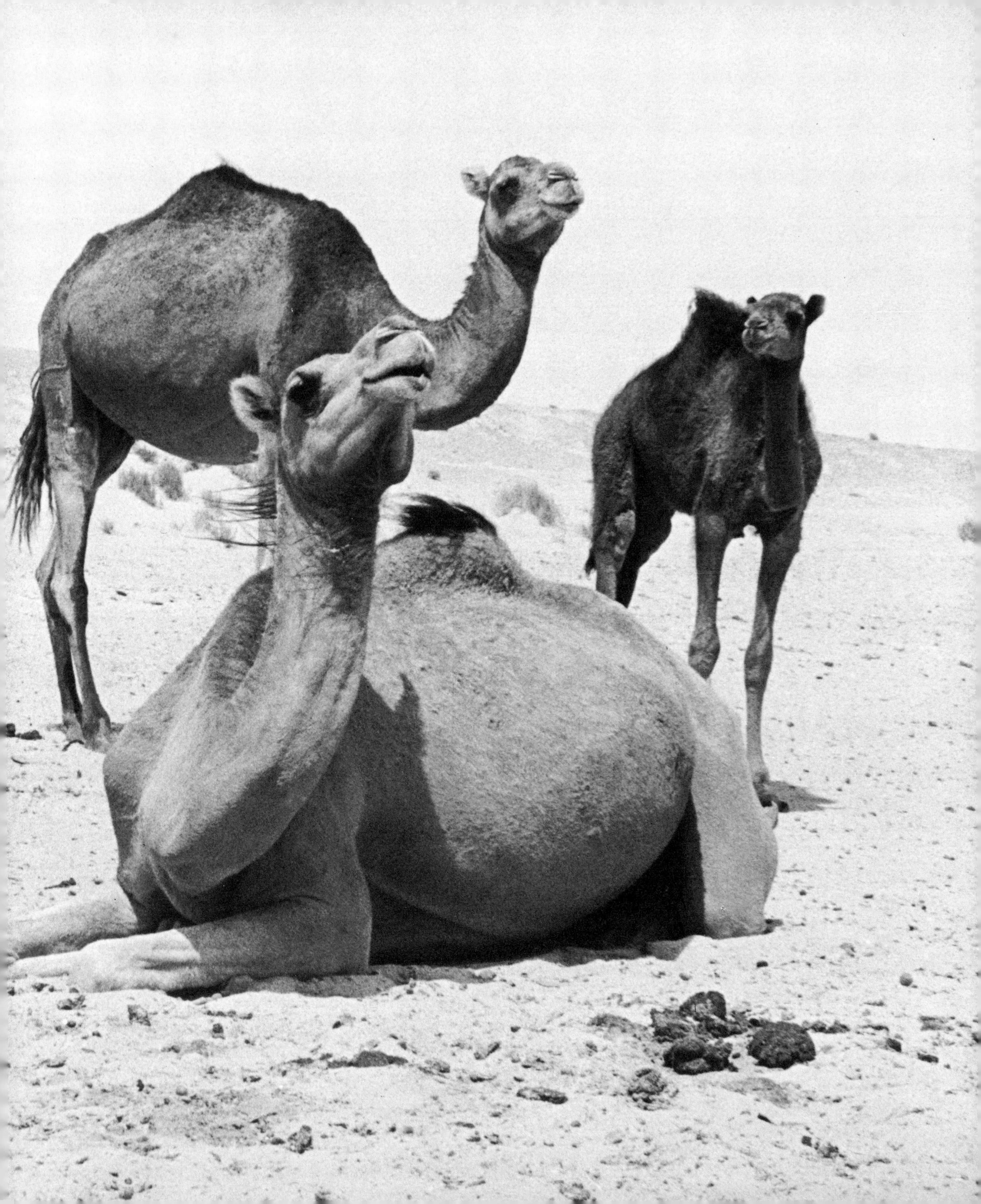

gence unit. Four-man patrols are sent out to scout, usually for two days at a time. The patrol usually consists of two Bedouin trackers, an Israeli soldier, and an Israeli commander. The Bedouins search for tracks and other signs of infiltration, and though tracked vehicles and helicopters might serve similar functions, they are noisy and consume huge quantities of fuel. The camel is quiet and can, if necessary, easily go through a two-day patrol without food or water. Furthermore, the camel is not likely to detonate a mine intended for tracked vehicles, and if he should detonate a personnel mine, his body would protect the soldier mounted high on his back. In military service the camel is treated well, but completely without sentiment. Even the Israeli soldiers, some of whom have dogs or other pets they're very fond of, seem to consider the camel no more than a necessary irritant.

Most camels, however, escape military service. Within a radius of one hundred miles in Tunisia, I saw camels pulling plows and carts, hauling water from wells, and carrying men and goods. I also saw a lot of them sleeping in the sun, but they were only waiting to pull or carry something or somebody. These camels all require training to do their jobs, and this is usually administered by the man who

The hay is not as heavy as it looks, but the camel will raise hell anyway.

The trainer trying to lead the camel.

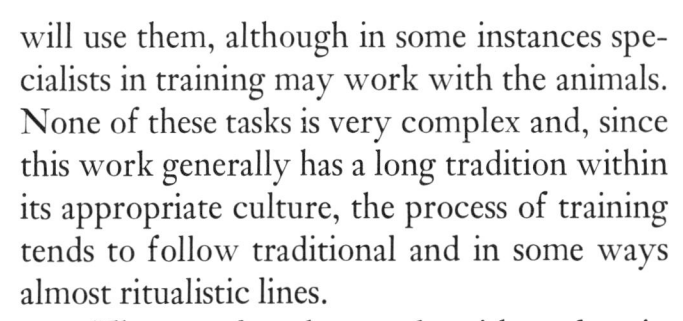

This camel is learning to sit on command.

will use them, although in some instances specialists in training may work with the animals. None of these tasks is very complex and, since this work generally has a long tradition within its appropriate culture, the process of training tends to follow traditional and in some ways almost ritualistic lines.

The people who work with and train camels are at least as interesting as the beasts themselves. At the time I was observing the Tunisian camels doing all those things, I made the acquaintance of a "chamelier." With his bent back, long scrawny neck, huge toucan nose, and plodding stride, he resembled his charges to a remarkable degree. He was also equally silent. He seemed especially remarkable to me because the camels respected him. Camels do not respect me. I don't know why, but any camel, given the chance, spits at me. At first I would approach them, as I approach any animal, with an open heart. I have since learned to approach with open eyes and wary tread. Initially, after wiping myself off, I took the spitting good-naturedly, but this was a mistake. The spitting wasn't meant good-naturedly, and when disregarded it was followed by attempted bites and kicks. Since I take pride in getting along with animals, this *affaire du chameau* still rankles. So I watched the ageless Bedouin grunt at his animals. He would holler at them hoarsely, slap them with a small branch, pull at their rope harness, and on one occasion I saw him twist a camel's upper lip painfully with the rope halter. They did as he wanted them to do. While I cannot say they were gracious about it, they did it. And they didn't spit, bite, or kick. He commanded in a surly manner and they obeyed in a surly manner, unfailingly. The whole procedure just wasn't my style of relating to animals, which, I suppose, is why I have my problems with camels.

The Bedouins recognize that camels show fear and anger, guilt, affection, pleasure, and sadness. Shimon says:

"When the camel stands with his head up and he walks out or runs, it means he's happy. He looks like a sick man when he's sad. He

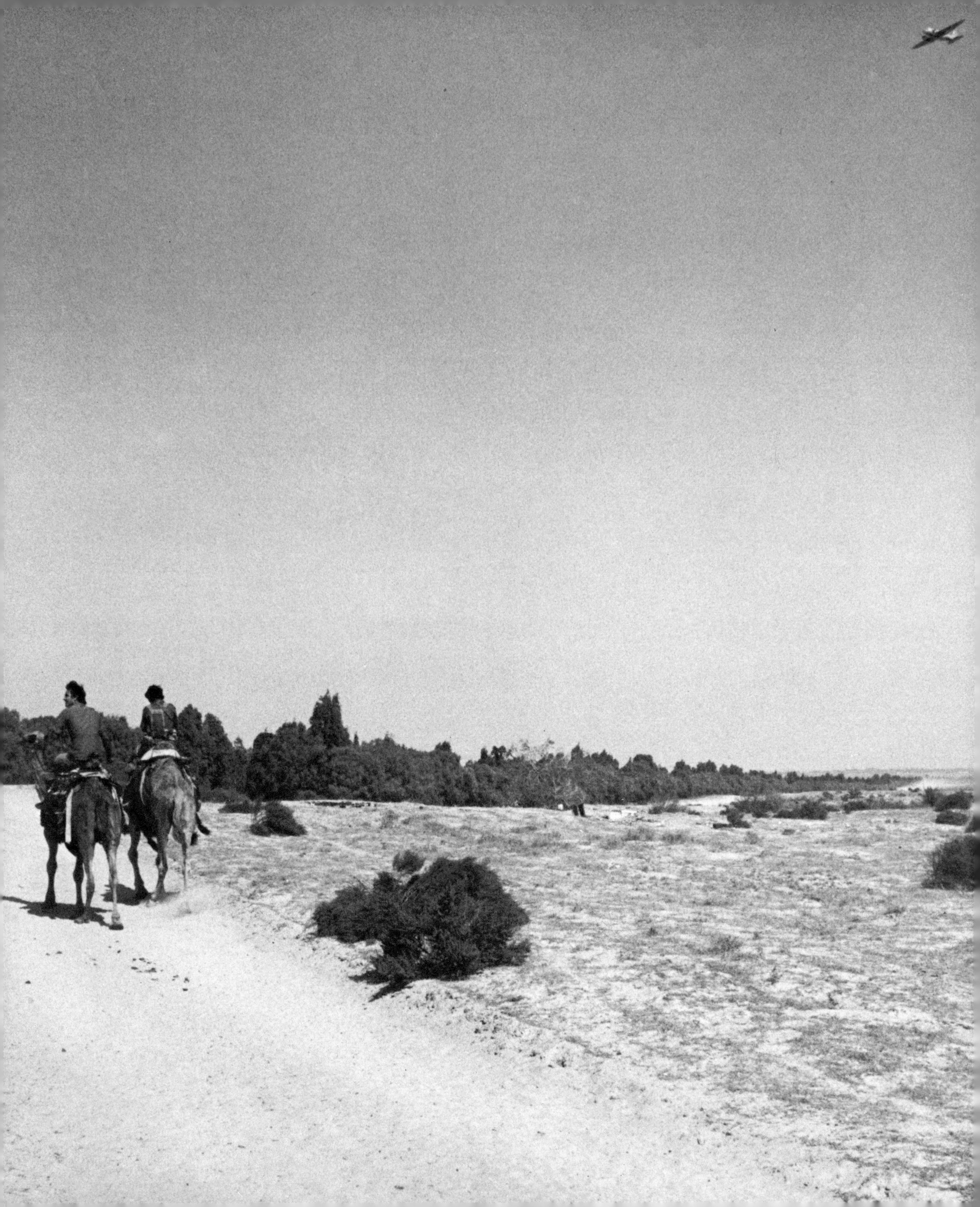

Which is the Jewish lieutenant and which the Arab tracker?

puts his head down. When he gets angry he's running away and does what he wants. The camel is tough. If he wants to sit down you cannot make him get up. If you make a fire under him he won't get up. When the camel does something wrong, how do you know it? You can't catch him. He's running away. He's frightened so he's running by himself because he knows that he did something wrong. Once during the winter his owner was sleeping beside him and he tied him, but not very well. So the camel, because this man was not very good to him, started biting him while he was sleeping. Fortunately, he was covered by blankets so the camel took only the blanket. When this man woke up this camel ran away and started traveling. The man was very frightened. And he couldn't catch the camel any more."

The camel is regarded by the Bedouins as very strong (they praise a man by saying he's "strong as a camel"), fleet of foot ("he goes faster than a jeep"), willful, vindictive, and endowed with exceptional hearing. There is a Bedouin saying:

> If you are in your tent and your camel makes noises of alarm, you must pack your belongings, fold your tent, load your camel, and leave. Somewhere in the distance danger approaches.
>
> If you are in your tent and your horse neighs in fright, get on the horse and leave.
>
> If you are in your tent and your dog barks a warning, run for your weapon.
>
> If you are in your tent and you hear your donkey bray, you have time only for a very short prayer.

Some people feel that the only good camel is a muzzled camel.

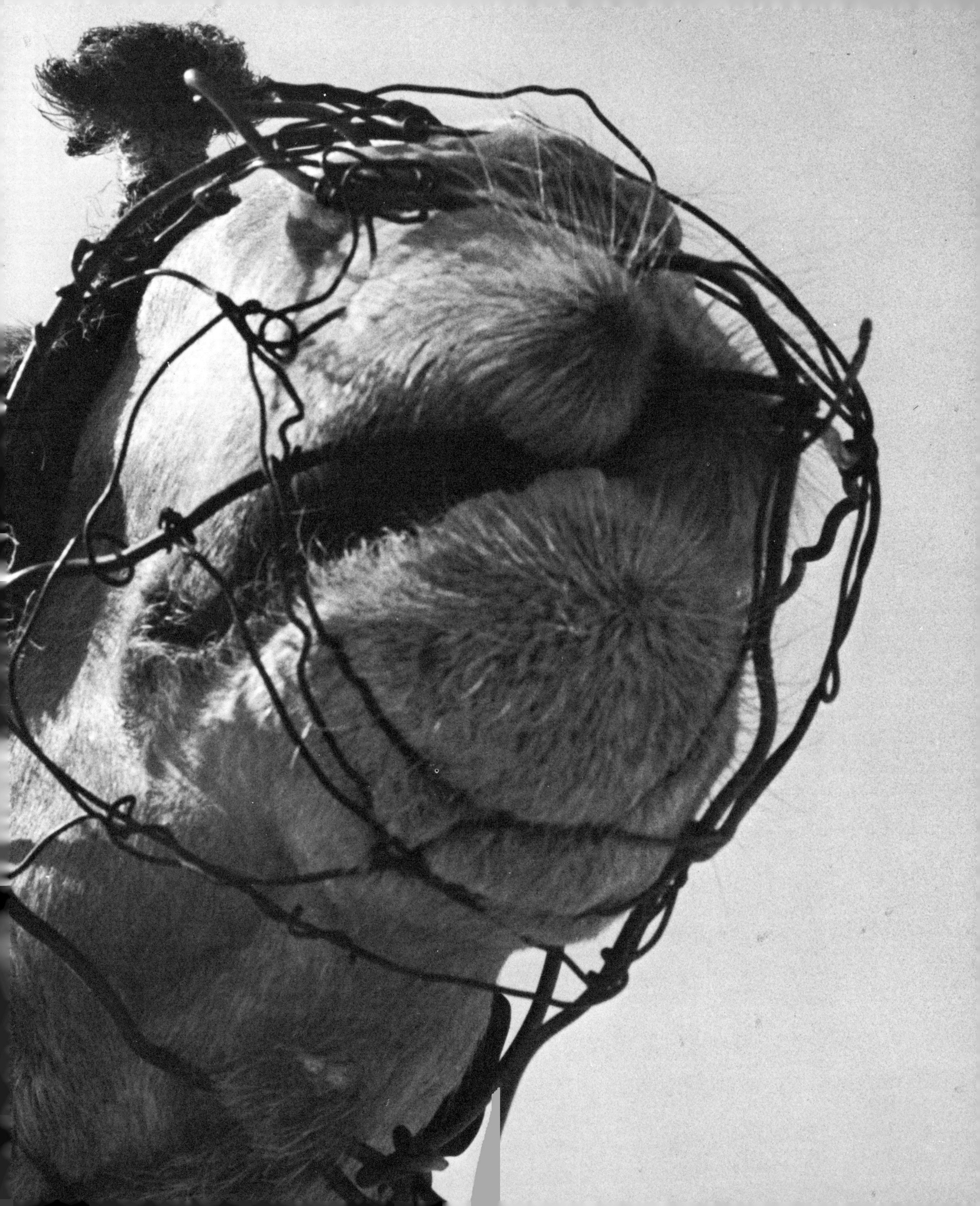

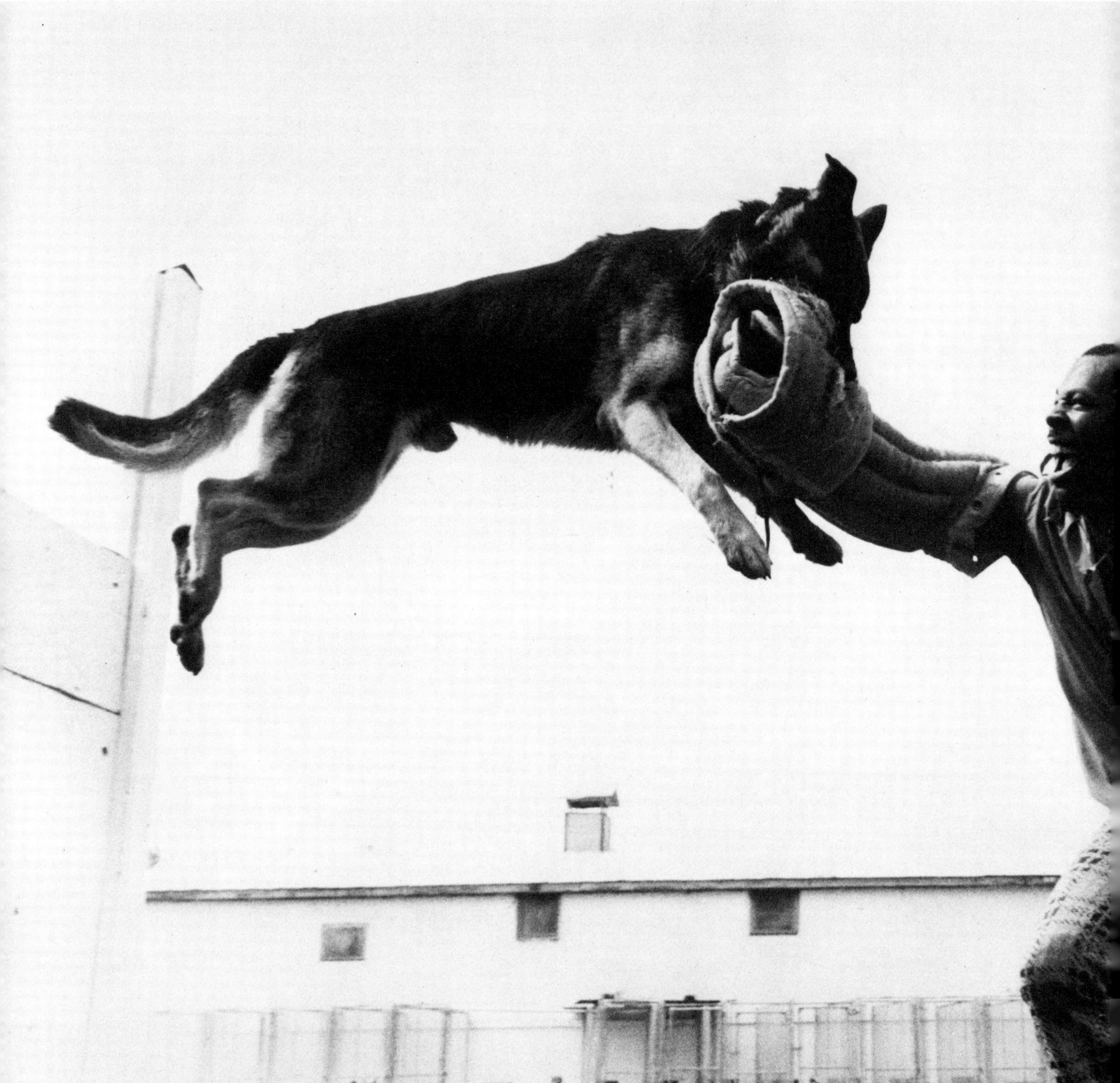

Cerberus

The dog with the prickly back, with the long and thin muzzle, the dog Vanghapata, which evil-speaking people call the Duzaka: this is the good creature among the creatures of the Good Spirit that from midnight till the sun is up goes and kills thousands of the creatures of the Evil Spirit.
—The Zendavesta

Benny was a sniffler. They used to ask him, "Benny, waddya snifflin'?" and Benny would say, "Nothin'." Now he had something to sniffle about. He was sitting on top of a pile of crates next to a warehouse and it was very cold and very dark. He used to like the dark, because it made him feel more comfortable, but he had been perched up there for an hour now and the chill wind was awful. Jordan, hunched up next to him, was no help at all. What a dumb name—"Jordan!" Well, Benny had his nose and Jordan had his name. Everybody's got his own hassles.

Moving lights pierced through the darkness of the street outside the warehouse yard. Benny and Jordan quickly yelled "Help!" at the top of their lungs, but the car went by heedlessly and the big dog at the foot of the crate pile bared his big white teeth viciously and growled.

"Ah, go home to ya mudda," Benny mumbled disconsolately.

"Ya shouldn' talk like that to him," Jordan said. "It puts him in a bad mood."

"He ain't puttin' me in no good mood, Jordan," Benny said, and mumbled to himself, " 'Jordan!' Fa' Chrissake, wadda name!"

On the ground below them the big German shepherd (who had the respectable name of Blitz) was tense, alert, and hostile. He made it clear that if he could get at them he'd eat them—period—and that, furthermore, he was prepared to wait forever. The gray trailer-trucks lined up in the yard looked, in the gloom, like hulks of primeval beasts, but they weren't nearly as menacing as Blitz.

"Y' c'n bet your ass I ain't doin' no more jobs with you, Benny," Jordan said. "You're too stupid."

Benny sniffled. "I tol' ya everythin' right. Them trucks is full of stuff. And I was right, there ain't even no watchman. An' I was right we could get in pretty easy."

"Sure, Benny," Jordan said. "We got in easy. You told me that! You suckered me into this like Little Red Ridin' Hood. Now talk to Gramma down there about how we're goin' to get out!"

Another car came into sight through the gloom, moving down the street at an unusually slow speed. Jordan started to shout, Benny joined in, and to their delight the slow-moving car ground to a halt!

"Hey! In here! Dis dog won' let us out!"

Benny turned to Jordan, whose eyes were glued to the rescue car. "See, Jordan? I tol' ya. Stick with Benny an' everythin' works out." Peering at Jordan for a look of approval, Benny saw the relief on his face slowly give way to dismay. He followed Jordan's eyes to the rescuers emerging from the car.

"Hey, Benny," Jordan said grimly, "y' like pigs better'n dogs?"

Benny watched the uniforms approach in the grim morning light. He sniffled.

One man's "best friend" can be another man's poison. Blitz was a business dog, one of those formidable canines whose profession it is to protect property. As in many professions, the hardest part of his job was the training period, but now that he's a professional his services are highly respected and much in demand. Truck-fleet owners in high-crime areas can lose fortunes until trained dogs are put in. The dogs usually cut the incidence of vandalism and thievery to zero. Unlike human watchmen, they don't sleep or drink on the job; they are constantly alert and their senses are remarkably keen. Furthermore, they are completely fearless, because they are trained to be so.

According to Captain Arthur Haggerty, who might well be the foremost guard-dog trainer in the country, "A well-trained attack-dog considers himself invincible. It just wouldn't occur to him to be afraid of any man. It's conceivable that such a dog could, with some difficulty, be shot. But it's inconceivable that he would be afraid of a man with a gun."

In Captain Haggerty's school a well-trained attack-dog has gone through a lot to get that way. Clients may send their own dogs for training, but Captain Haggerty prefers to select his own dogs, train them, and sell them. Many of his dogs are German shepherds he has acquired on buying trips to Germany. The first step is conventional obedience training. This introduces the dog to schooling, teaches him obedience and precision, and provides the trainer-trainee pair the opportunity to adapt to each other's personality. If a dog shows particular aptitude, he graduates to the level of attack training. This usually begins with the help of an assistant who teases the leashed dog with a piece of burlap sacking, taunting him or yelling at him at the same time. The trainer shouts at the dog, encouraging him to attack the cloth. This teasing lasts about thirty seconds. The moment the dog makes any response, however slight, he is praised and the assistant runs off as if he were frightened.

One of the major principles of Captain Haggerty's training technique is the constant effort to build a dog's confidence. During the entire training process the dog *always* wins. In every exercise where the dog is confronted by a mock intruder or assailant, the exercise always ends with the antagonist running away. Even if the dog's response is only a flicker of interest, the interloper runs. Of course, the dog is encouraged to make increasingly vigorous responses, since Captain Haggerty is by no means satisfied with "a flicker of interest."

When the dog gets the general idea and regularly attacks the burlap, he is ready for the next step. The dog is placed on the alert by the handler's command "Watch him!" and the intruder-assistant appears, this time with the sacking wrapped around his arm (over plenty of padding). The trainer orders the dog to attack and the brouhaha starts. Again the dog is praised for any response he makes, and the assistant runs away. The final step in this series of lessons is to replace the sacking with a "civilian sleeve," which is an ordinary jacket or coat worn over a protective plastic splint. The dog learns to attack the coated arm on command, just as he did with the arm wrapped in sacking.

The chief factors in this process are the building up of confidence and of tension, which results in a direct attack on the assistant. During the training, however, the dog always remains under the trainer's control. In teaching him to be aggressive on command, the trainer must excite and stimulate the dog, but not to the point where there's any chance of his losing complete control of the animal. A great trainer must therefore have great artistry and sensitivity. The effectiveness of the training depends on his accurate assessment of the dog's temperament and personality and his ability to control the dog's motivation and behavior.

Theoretically, any dog can be attack-trained. Practically speaking, however, certain breeds are favored because of their physical and psychological characteristics. Although Macy's department store and many other firms use Dobermans, Captain Haggerty strongly favors German shepherds. Many other breeds are also used. I once saw a Bouvier de Flandres demonstrate a series of complex aggressive training exercises that were more impressive than any I've since encountered.

Aside from breed characteristics, the individual qualities of the dog should match the job for which he's destined. For example, a dog who's going to be on guard patrol should have a strong territorial instinct. Special jobs often have special requirements. Some men once came to Captain Haggerty from a neighboring state to inquire about attack-training. They asked, among other things, some questions about the dog's collar. The captain is a smart man, and he has had enough experience to spot an unusual question. He realized that these men wanted a dog who would attack any stranger who touched its collar. Apparently, trained dogs aren't the only ones who can sniff out smuggled narcotics. In addition to being smart and experienced, Captain Haggerty is also big—very big. He threw the guys out.

On another occasion a man whose job it was to collect rents in a tough neighborhood wanted a dog to help him feel secure at his work. "Well, a guy's entitled to do his legitimate work," said the captain, "so I got him a dog and we started training. It was going along fine, and both the dog and the man were getting more and more enthusiastic. But after a while I got the uneasy feeling that the man was *too* enthusiastic. He'd get into the spirit of the thing and he'd start yelling at the dog, 'Kill him! Tear the bastard to pieces! Tear his arm off!' It was eerie. It got so scary I finally said to the guy, 'I'm sorry—we'll have to knock it off. I can't give you the dog!'

"So he went away but he called me on the phone and started threatening me. 'I'm gonna come up there and kick your ass off,' he said. 'Well,' I said, 'there's no anchor on your foot and no fence around my ass. You know where to find me.' He never showed up, but I found out about him later. He was in the real-estate business like he said—but not quite like he said. He was a guy landlords would hire when they wanted to get tenants out of those slum buildings. And he got them out. That's what he wanted the dog to help him do."

Most of Captain Haggerty's customers are, of course, legitimate businessmen who want to protect their business property or householders who want to protect their homes. "We rent out a lot of business dogs," he told me. "They may take care of the dogs, or we may deliver them in the evening and then pick them up in the morning after work. But when

Theoretically, any dog can be trained for attack work.

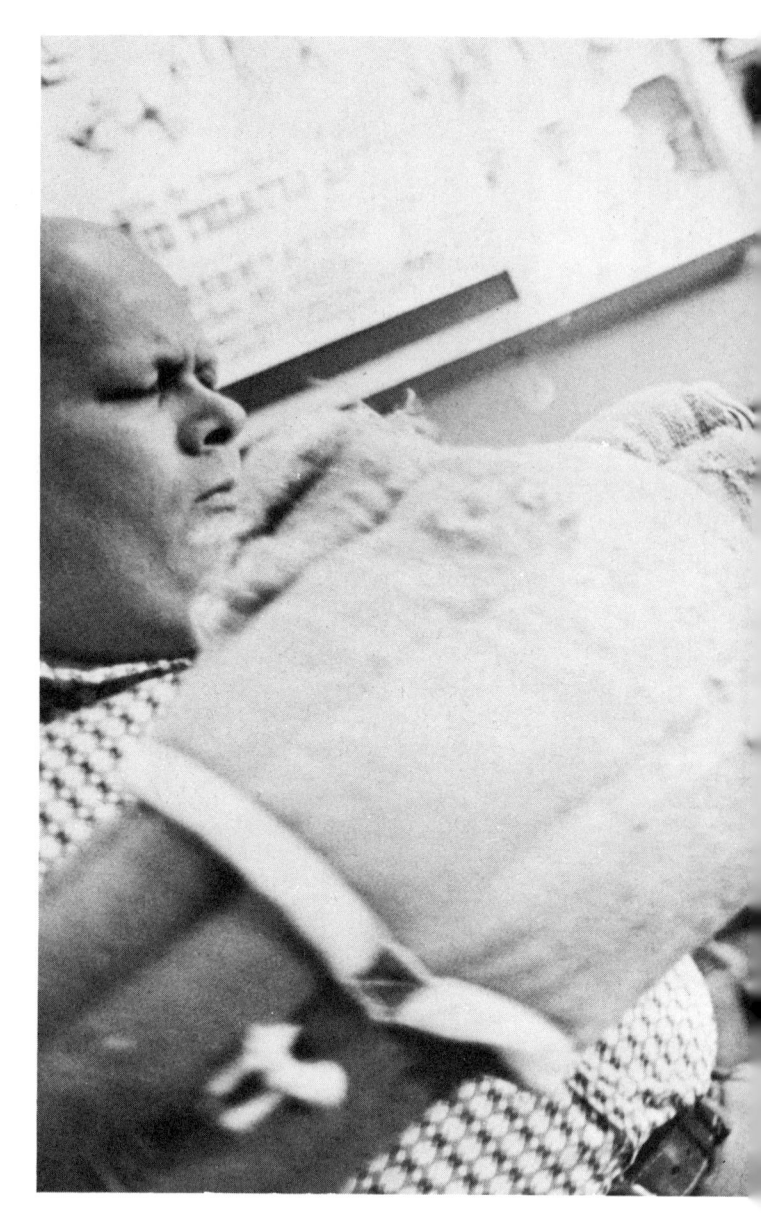

a lady calls up and wants to rent a dog in her home just for a day or two, I don't even bother. I already know what it's all about. She's recently divorced and she's expecting her ex-husband to come around, maybe to pick up the kids for the day. She's hoping that dog will slice up her husband when he shows."

It's obvious from his stories that Captain Haggerty is keenly aware of the fact that his dogs are potentially lethal weapons. Their use is not regulated by law, so he has a big ethical responsibility. Somehow, he has to be able to

The trainer should be at least as alert as the dog.

tell the difference between people who want attack dogs for defensive reasons and those who want to use them aggressively.

Obviously, there are two ends to that leash. As I said, each dog has its own combination of qualities that constitute his temperament. He (or she) may be relatively aggressive or shy, excitable or placid, friendly or aloof, and so on. The trainer must accurately assess and instinctively adapt to these qualities. But he (or she) will do so in his own way, according to his own personality. The trainer also may be aggressive or shy, excitable or placid, friendly or aloof. Captain Haggerty characterizes the good trainer-dog relationship as a professional one. He will develop a kind of respect for and appreciation of a dog who works well with him, but he makes a point of differentiating that from the affection he feels for his house pets.

"A trainer can't afford to fall in love with the dog he's working with. He would lose objectivity. When that happens he doesn't see the dog's limitations, his weak points. He begins to make excuses for the dog. I have to keep my student trainers working with lots of dogs so they don't get too attached to one dog. They're not supposed to be hard on the dogs, but they must be consistently firm and clear. I have to keep reminding them that the dog's welfare, and even its life, or the life of some human being, may depend on the effectiveness of the training.

"There are all kinds of students, but the one thing they have in common is that they like dogs. I have to make sure they realize that if they're wishy-washy in their correction they're *not* being kind to the dog. And sometimes I have to give them pretty graphic descriptions of what could happen. I've even gone so far in dealing with this problem as to tell some students who are getting out of line that the dog they're falling for is going to be destroyed after the training. I don't think they believe me, but it does hold them down. These are dog lovers I'm working with."

A good dog trainer, then, has to have professional objectivity and he has to have confidence. He can't afford to get too anxious even though his professional reputation rests with each dog he trains. He can't afford to be afraid of failure, and he can't afford to be afraid of the dog. A quick-moving dog capable of vicious attack is a formidable playmate, and it must be trained to the point that its trainer has utterly confident control. But up to that point there's always *some* element of unpredictability. Captain Haggerty and his student trainers frequently joke about being bitten. Their jokes signal an underlying anxiety. The Captain says, "Sure I've been bitten. But I've never had lacerations, only puncture wounds. A dog trainer can't afford to lose his cool no matter what. Even if you're being bitten you have to keep enough control that you don't pull away and tear yourself to pieces."

Captain Haggerty made it clear that while dogs serve a lot of human needs, those needs are sometimes conflicting. In order to have an effective relationship with a dog, one must know what one's needs are, i.e., what is the essential point of the relationship. If it's a working relationship, forget the love. If we turn that around, however, can we say that the opposite is valid: If it's a loving relationship forget the work? Captain Haggerty believes that if your relationship with a dog is basically motivated by love, you're not going to have a serious working dog. You may get him to do useful things, but he'll never be a professional dog like Blitz. There are other kinds of work besides guarding that dogs do for humans. Take sled dogs, for example. It's possible to teach the dog you love to pull a sled, but it will always be fundamentally a sport for him, as it is for you. He'll be an amateur but never a professional sled-puller. What about dogs that are trained to guide the blind? Surely this is one working relationship that must include love. Without going into details of that type of training, we need only realize that a person whose life depends on that dog can afford to be loving only when the pair are not working. Even then the blind person needs to be certain that the dog knows the difference between working and playing.

Trainers tell of people who bring their

dogs to a school, or acquire dogs from a school, and train with them for some work, let's say protecting their own home. Too often the story goes: "He got this great dog. He learned how to alert the dog, get him to hold someone off, get him to attack, get him to release, all these great things. He put out all this money and time and effort. And you know what he did? He took the dog home and made a goddamn pet out of him. He ruined him!"

Of course the dog wasn't ruined. It's just that he was trained to be a work dog and ended up serving as a pet. He was ruined for the job his owner thought he wanted the dog to do. He could no longer be a professional guard dog, but he was probably a great pet. The owner didn't realize that he wanted a pet rather than a professional guard dog, or else he didn't know that you can't have both in one dog.

Most people who want a hybrid, a working pet, have to compromise. The more serious the emotional involvement, the less serious the work. There can, of course, be some of each. Most of the work that pets do they do because they've been taught a "trick" or because they are motivated to do something that just happens to be something you want them to do. An example of the former is the dog who's been taught to carry the grocery bag or pull a child's wagon. Pets who are thought of as watch dogs by their owners are those who bark or attack strangers who come into the house. But they're barking or attacking because they are inwardly moved to do so, perhaps out of a fear of strangers or because of a natural territorial instinct. They won't bark or attack dependably or stop barking or attacking consistently when *you* want them to. Your pet may do a useful thing by barking

when strangers come near, but he's by no means a working dog on that account. The big issue is reliability. You simply can't rely in an emergency on a dog that hasn't been trained and maintained as a professional in a specific job.

Even the rescue stories one reads don't contradict that basic fact. If a dog is motivated to do something that saves someone's life, that's very lucky. If it was my life, I'd be very grateful indeed. But I wouldn't depend on it the next time. Because I don't know and don't have complete control of what made him do what he did, and some key factor may be missing next time. All the dogs in movies and on television who do that sort of thing are carefully trained to do precisely that—on cue.

54

If the movie makes it look as if they're doing it for love, it's a hoax. I do believe that a dog's love can be relied on, but I don't believe that what he'll do on account of that love can be dependably predicted.

Dependability, that's the mark of the pro. In this chapter I've tried to describe the training of working dogs, but I don't mean to discourage pet owners. On the contrary, I hope that what I've said makes you a little more understanding and accepting if you haven't been able to train your pet to the peak of efficiency in this or that. You've probably struck just the right balance by teaching your dog to adapt well enough to your way of life so that you're both free to love each other. Few people really want to make the training such a heavy thing that it will interfere with that relationship.

Sometimes a professional dog trainer—who usually has a pet of his own—speaks quizzically of pet owners: "I don't know what it is. If you're tactful about it, you can sometimes point out to a man some flaw in his wife. He'll say, 'Yeah, but she's a wonderful mother and a terrific cook.' You might even be able to criticize his kids. But hint that his dog has some weakness? No way! A guy will come in with a four-year-old dog and want me to teach him how to train the dog. I ask myself why, after all this time, he suddenly decides he needs to learn how to handle the dog. I look at the bandage on the guy's arm and the fresh scar on his face and I ask the guy, 'Do you have any special problems with the dog?' Nope, no problems. He just wants to obedience-train the dog. No kind of torture is going to make that guy admit that his dog turns on him. When people talk about dog's loyalty to man, send 'em to me. I'll tell a few stories about man's loyalty to dog!"

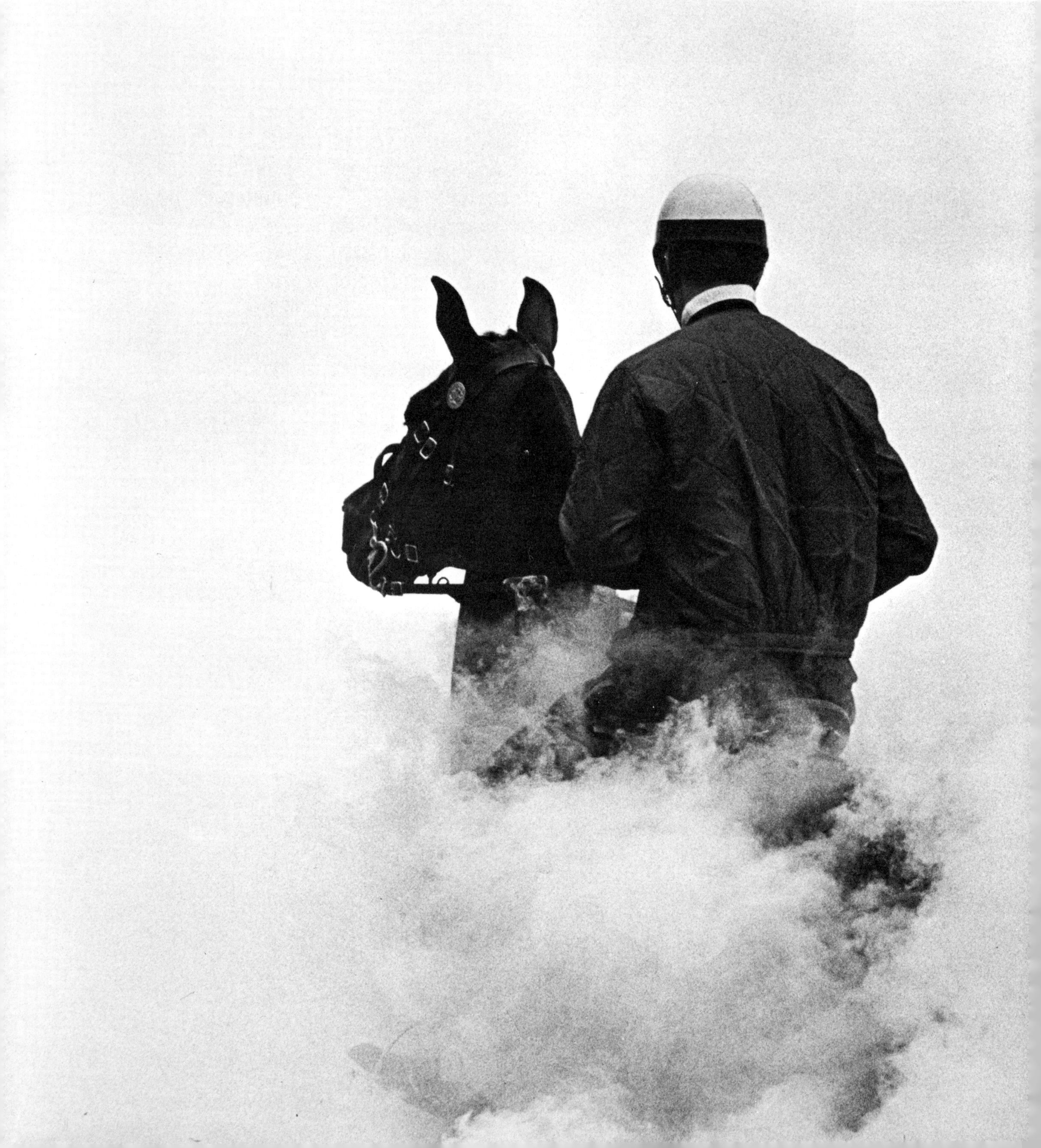

Old Gray Mares Need Not Apply

He saith among the trumpets, Ha, ha! and he smelleth the battle afar off, the thunder of the captains, and the shouting.
—Job XXXIX, 25

Lieutenant Caspar of the New York City Mounted Police Troop has a guardian angel. Because the lieutenant has had more narrow escapes than Evel Knievel, it has always been obvious that he has had someone looking out for him. At one point he actually *saw* his guardian angel.

"I bent down to tie my shoelace. I had a placid mount, so I let go of the reins. I shouldn't have done that. He took off down the road like he was fulfilling an old ambition. I stood there for a moment just to taste the ashes as I watched my career, my future, my life disappearing lickety-split into the sunset. Then I started running. I was like a crazy man—running, yelling, waving my arms, crying big tears. Well, man, this was New York! Sure enough, that old horse goin' like hell *down* the road was heading awful fast for a truck comin' *up* the road. I went completely insane. Then I saw that truck jerk to a stop. A big guy jumped down, ran to the middle of the street, planted himself right in front of that charging horse, and started to wave his arms and yell. You wouldn't believe it, but that horse went into low gear and wasn't sure he wanted any of that road at all. The guy grabbed the reins and waited while I came puffing up. I said, "Jeez, mister, what can I do for you? Can I give you a present? Can I give you money? Can I give you my life?'

"'No,' he says, 'it's okay. Any time!' And he jumps in the truck and takes off. It wasn't until about five minutes later it hit me. 'Holy boob,' I says to myself. 'Who would expect to find an angel driving a truck?'"

It's tough for a mounted patrolman to be separated from his mount. They have both been through a lot together: a long, hard period of training, working day in and day out on the streets of New York, in refresher training courses, riots, strikes, traffic, parades, all kinds of crime, and even the National Horse Show. Lieutenant Caspar is commander of Troop A in the Bronx, where the re-mount depot is, which means that all training of New York City policemen and horses is done in his bailiwick. Most of the actual training is done by two patrolmen, Walter Fink and Dennis Byrnes, who are the two most knowledgeable horsemen in the unit. But the job calls for much more than knowledge. It requires skill, ingenuity, tact, and the ability to communicate effectively with both horses and men. I should say "men and women," for there are a number of women in the mounted unit of the auxiliary police, and they too come to Walter and Dennis for training. So for that matter do the mounted units of a number of other police departments in the New York area.

For both men and animals the major part of the schooling is in basic horsemanship, although the most interesting activities have to do with specific police work. Compared to policemen in cars or on foot, mounted patrolmen have the advantage of visibility and greater mobility. Perhaps their greatest value is in crowd control. For this they must learn hand signals and special formations. The "wedge," for example, is a means of separating a crowd into handleable segments; the "hollow square" is used to protect people or vehicles that are being extricated from a trouble area.

Police horses have problems that other horses rarely face. It's hard to guess what will spook a horse, but a congested city offers an infinite number of possibilities. When the horses are trained, therefore, they and their riders must be subjected to all sorts of unexpected traumas so that they can go out on patrol confident in each other's reactions. Noise is one major factor. Walter and Dennis, under Lieutenant Caspar, have devised all sorts of techniques to simulate problems that might arise. They have rigged up an amplifier system to a record player that blares out a variety of city noises as well as some raucous parade music. At any moment a quiet ride around the ring may be interrupted by pistol shots. Or Lieutenant Caspar will stroll casually into the ring, produce a closed umbrella from behind his back, and pop it open in a horse's face. He likes spray cans, too. He will lounge against the barrier surrounding the ring and call out to a passing patrolman, "Hey—c'mere." The officer will edge his mount over to the lieutenant and both horse and rider will be met by a squirt of perfume. The horses sometimes swear at the lieutenant, but the men just hang on grimly and occasionally manage a kind of sickly grin. The lieutenant becomes soothing and talks kindly to the pair: "Aw, c'mon. It's nothing. Just a can. C'mere—look at the can. See? It can't hurt you. Just a little old can. It makes a nice smell [squirting the can in the opposite direction]. See? Nothin' to it." The horse looks suspicious, the rider determinedly impassive. "C'mon over here again and look at it good. C'mon, horse, I'm the lieutenant. You gotta do what I say [squirting spray in the horse's face]. See—it can't hurt you."

Although the mounted-police horses are stabled all over the city, it all started in Central Park. The 1871 Annual Report of the Police Department explains how the mounted unit came into being:

> Since the avenues leading to and beyond the Central Park have been laid with wood and other smooth pavements, and for that reason have become crowded with vehicles, there has grown up a practice, by a certain class of persons, of fast and reckless driving through these much frequented thoroughfares, at rates of speed perilous to the lives and property of themselves and more prudent and orderly citizens.
>
> This reprehensible practice, though dangerous and unlawful, could not be prevented nor the offending parties arrested, by a police patrol moving on foot. With a view to a more complete suppression of this rapidly growing evil, the Board, by resolutions adopted on the 10th day of July, 1871, established a horse patrol, called "The Mounted Police Squad No. 1," to cover the avenues in question.
>
> The services of the squad have been thorough, and eminently useful. . . . This service has reduced the casualties and injuries, from fast and reckless driving, to such an extent, that the avenues in question, can now be used by orderly and quiet citizens, with a degree of comfort and safety not hitherto in recent years enjoyed.

Many horses and mounted patrolmen have "covered the avenues" since that time. A police-department brochure gives a picture of the horses and men one hundred years later. Here are some relevant excerpts.

> The horse must be intelligent, possessing quality, good conformation and a kind disposition. It must be tractable and quiet enough to be shod without difficulty. It should have an easy gait with

free and prompt action at walk, trot and gallop, free from any vices, with no unsightly brands and be of a type that is suitable for mounted police service. . . . During his probationary period he is subjected to many tests for soundness, docility and intelligence. If the horse meets these tests, he is finally accepted, becomes a part of the Police Department, and is given a name and number. . . .

His training and schooling is started and continued for a period of approximately 3 to 4 months. . . . Further education and training is necessary until the horse is almost fool-proof and can meet up with most conditions that might confront him and the rider on patrol. The training requires a great deal of untiring patience and common sense on the part of the trainers and handlers. It is attained by kindness and patience from all whom the horse comes into contact with.

Horses are assigned to mounted men usually over long periods of time. Constant association with each forms a

The wedge.

Rescuing a car.

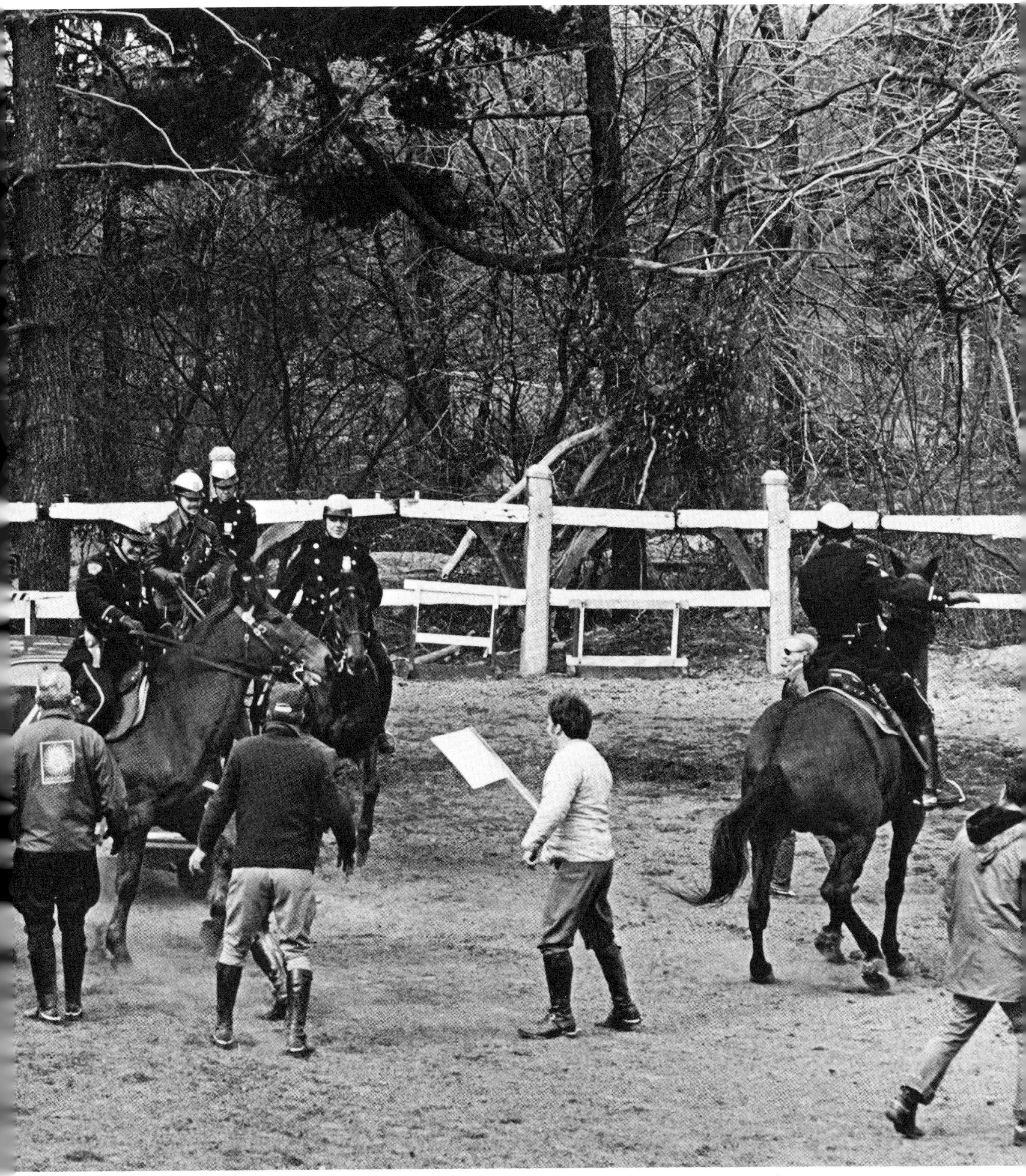

bond of companionship hard to break, and gives an understanding of the character of both man and horse. It is common knowledge among mounted members that a police horse has been known to pine, lose weight from lack of appetite, and go into a physical decline when his rider retired, or departed from his horse for other reasons. Similar emotional upsets have been experienced by the rider when he loses his horse through retirement or otherwise. . . .

Mounted recruits are drawn from police officers assigned to the various precincts. They must possess necessary physical qualifications. . . . They need not have any previous knowledge of horsemanship—just the desire to love and care for the animal as a parent does with its child.

As one might guess from the use of the masculine pronoun, these horses are all male—in fact, they must all be geldings "of a certain age"—past the lighthearted years of adolescence and short of old age, although many horses remain with the troop well into their twenties before retirement to the city's farm in upper New York state. Geldings (or castrated males) are nearly always more tractable than stallions or mares, which are less predictable in stress-provoking situations. Size and color are not as important as age and sex, but they are considerations, too. Traditionally—for the sake of appearance in parade work—police horses had to be bay in color (red-brown with black mane and tail) and about 15½ hands (62 inches at the withers) in height. Because horses of the proper temperament are not manufactured in uniform shapes and colors like automobiles, and because parade work is less important now than police work, these standards have become more or less flexible, although you'll never see an old gray mare carrying a patrolman.

Lieutenant Caspar talked with me about the relationship of horse and rider. He pointed out that after a horse has been in the streets of New York for a while he's seen it all. He then becomes known as "a good street horse," and his man will come to work in the morning knowing that his horse won't dump him. It's the same for the horse. No matter what he has to put up with all day, he knows that it will pass and that when the time comes his rider will get him back to eat. Even so, some horses are highstrung. "We have one like that here but we know he isn't dangerous because the man who rides him likes him and sticks up for him. So the horse responds to him. We use our horses the way we use our sticks, as psychological weapons. I never saw a mounted officer use a stick. It just doesn't occur to him. In the same way, we never use the horse aggressively. If a crowd of people really knew horses, we might not be able to control them, but people respond to what they see as an unthinking hulk bearing down on them. In some situations that mounted officer has the power of ten foot-patrolmen."

As we were talking, Dennis, who was about to go back on patrol duty, came over to us. "I like patrol work. My horse and I know Orchard Beach well, and that's where we're going. He'll take me around and I can see what's going on. He's got a nose for booze. If he thinks there's some drinking going on in Beach Thirteen, the Puerto Rican beach, he'll take me there. If a Puerto Rican girl goes for coffee and an Italian man from Beach Twelve

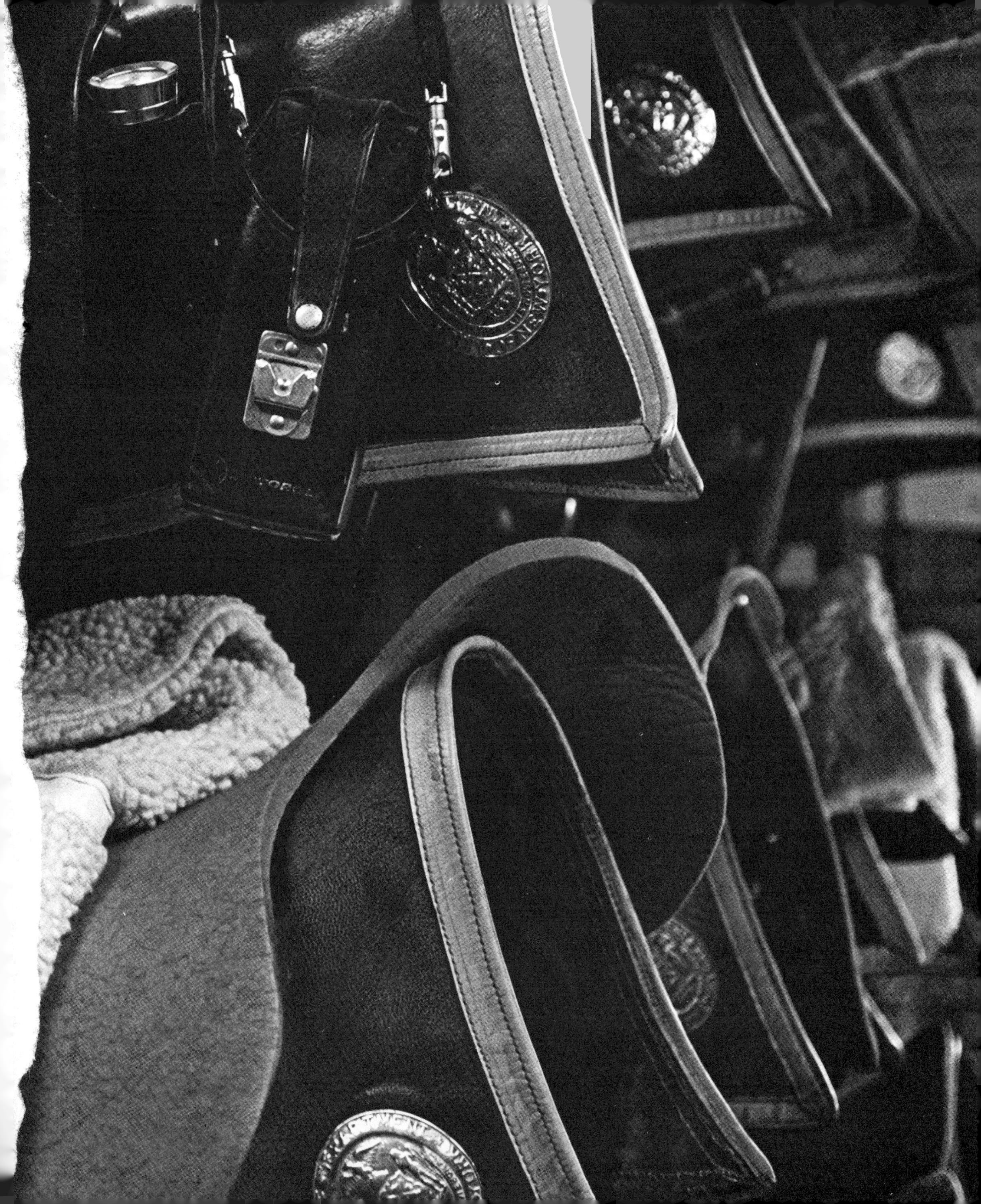

The horse must become accustomed to gunfire.

An amplifier blares out city noises.

The lieutenant likes spray cans.

loudly admires her, I can see the group of men on Beach Thirteen start to head for Twelve. And I can make sure they see me. Then there's the Divorced-and-Separated beach. The women there are always losing their car keys or their kids. I like that, because you get a chance to meet a lot of nice people and help them out. You put a lost kid up on the horse with you and everybody can see him and he's having the thrill of his life. He stops crying right away and he doesn't start again until his mom finds him and he has to get off the horse."

Walter chimed in: "Yeah, it's good to patrol on a horse. Everybody sees you, all kinds of things come up, and you gotta use your judgment. Every moment you have to be alert. Nothing goes exactly by the book. You see a little problem, you gotta keep it little. You see a big problem and you gotta *make* it little. And you have to adapt fast. When you stop a car for a routine check, you have to keep in mind that old people get frightened when a cop stops their car. And you have to be careful when kids are in the car. They get scared for their daddy and you must be respectful to their daddy. You never bawl out a driver or give a ticket to a man if his kid is listening. But if a guy gives you a hard time or acts tough, you gotta come down on him very hard and very fast. You may want to be a nice guy, but in some neighborhoods if you try to be nice they think you're scared and they bust your ass."

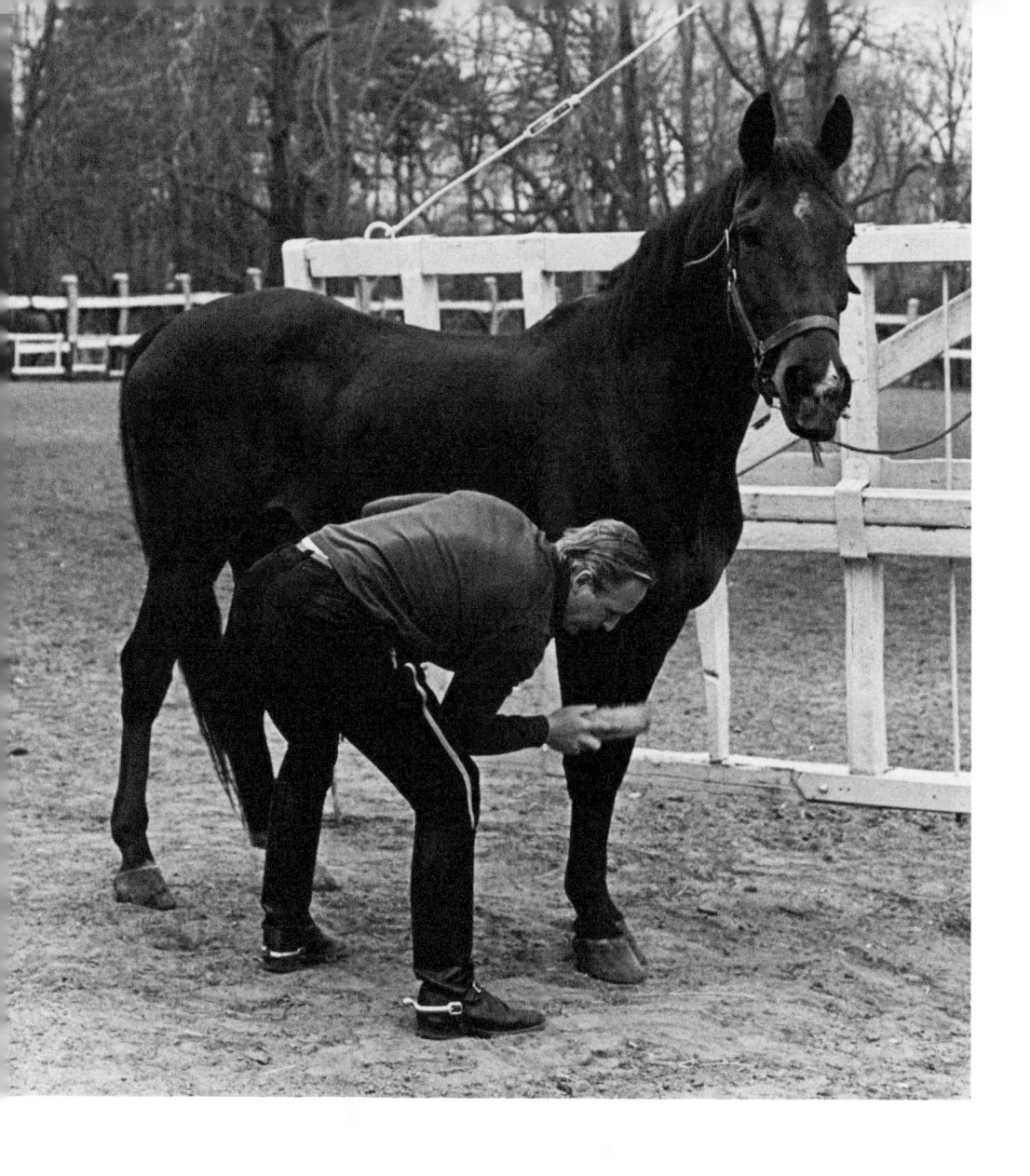

An officer had just come out of the locker room buttoning his tunic. "You know, I spent nine years in Bedford-Stuyvesant. Then they transferred me to Queens Village. At first it just seemed strange—like I had suddenly landed in a foreign country. The people would see the horse, smile at us, and say 'Hello!' That made my horse very nervous. He didn't know what to make of it. The first time a teen-age kid waved at me, I thought he was brandishing a knife. Some guy would stop to pass the time of day and the horse and I would get all tense wondering what he was up to. One guy got a heart attack and fell down in the street. I sent out a call for radio cars, because I figured it was a trap and that he had a grenade hidden under his belly. But after I'd been here a while I started to relax. Not the horse, though. He knew better. He had been through hell and he learned how to get me through it, but he's never learned how to deal with this. But I don't pay much attention to his nervousness and I get all loose and calm and dopey-like. When that happens, though, some little old lady, weighing about a hundred pounds, entices you down off your mount, slaps you with a crowbar, and you're layin' in the hospital trying to figure out what the hell it's all about. When you come out of the hospital, you find out that they sent your horse to re-mount and that all the auxiliaries are riding him. You go to rescue him but he won't give you the time of day. He says, 'Screw you, buddy! After ten years, you wouldn't listen to me and you screwed us both up—now get lost!'"

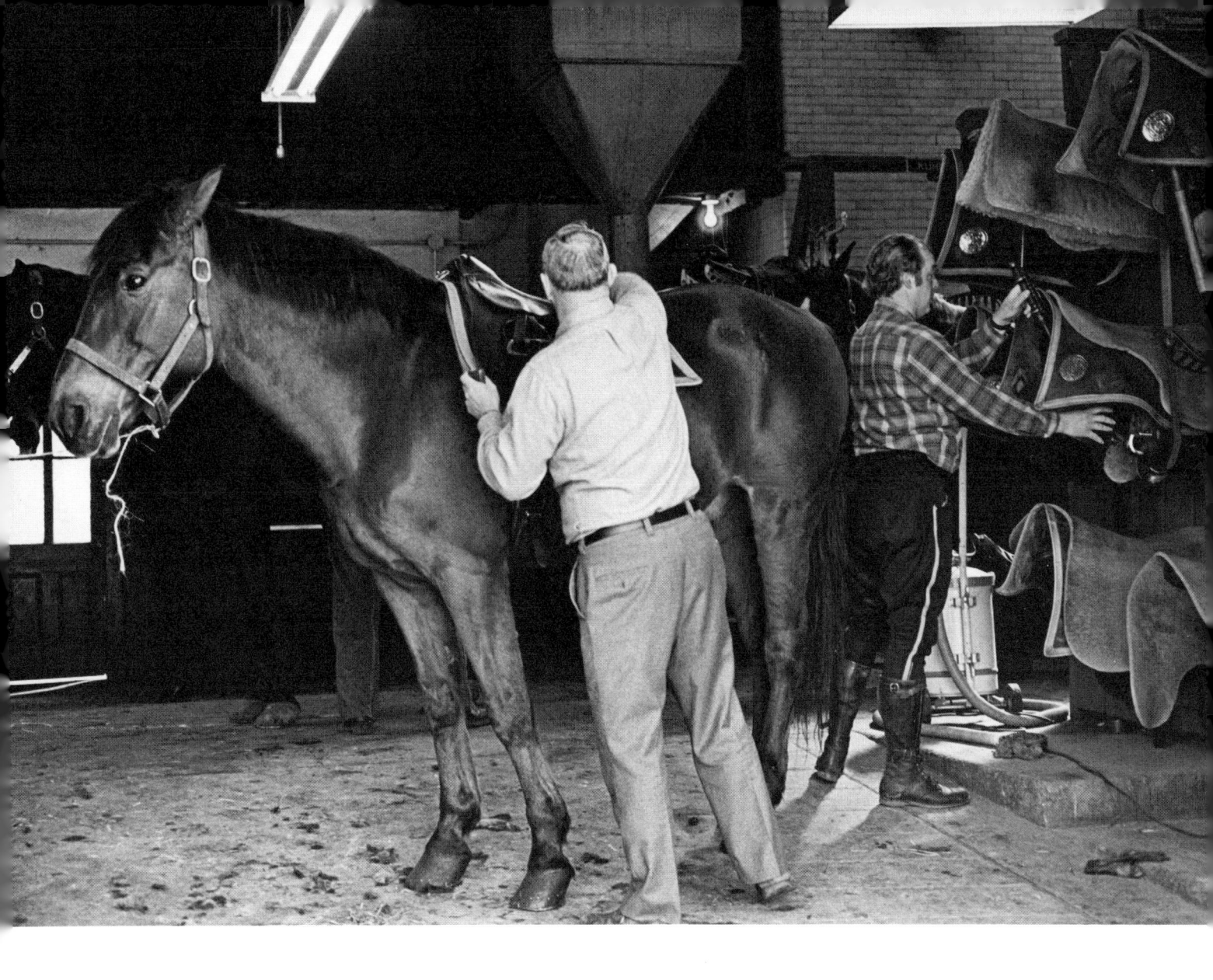

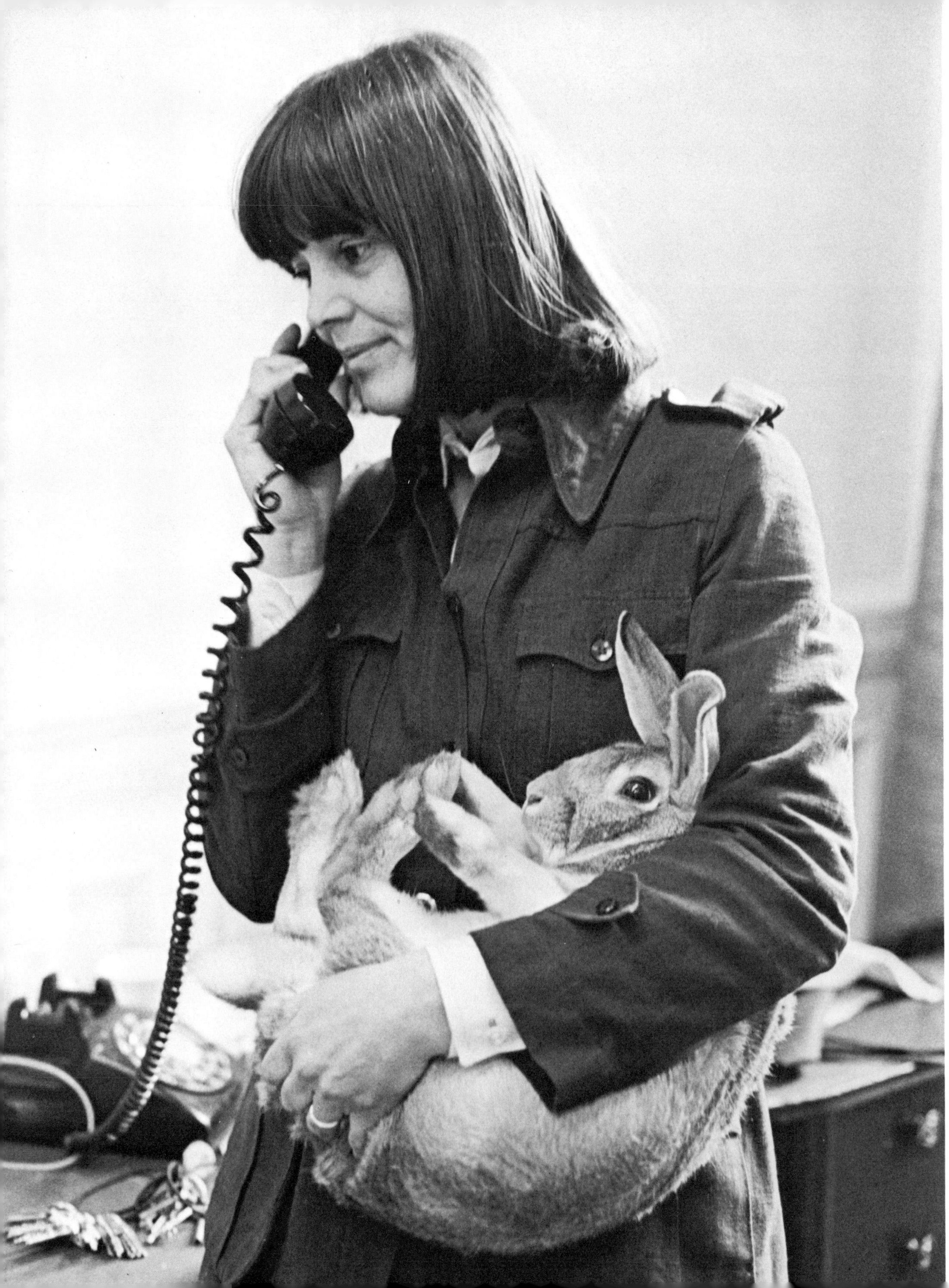

The Norman Conquest

*Ask now the beasts,
and they shall teach thee.*
—Job XII, 7

Norman is a rabbit with character. Unlike your average rabbit (who is, after all, just a rabbit), Norman is a rabbit with a mission. He is one of those dedicated creatures whose life style exudes high purpose. Norman is a teacher—or better, an educator. I make the distinction because he does not impart factual information. His style is rather to make one think, to give pause. He works in a large nursery school in Manhattan. That's far from unusual. No self-respecting nursery school in New York would be caught dead without an animal. Norman was acquired for the avowed purpose of teaching the children gentleness, responsibility to others, kinship with living things. He's been working there over a year now and he's not—how to say it?—an unmixed blessing.

There was, for example, the mother of a three-year-old who wondered: "Isn't it confusing to have a rabbit in a school with the name Merricat's Castle? My Susie thinks the school is named after Norman and therefore only animals with long ears are cats. Is that educational?" Or the indignant mother who suddenly found out why her two-year-old always had to have a snack the minute school was over: "One day I walked behind him as he went into his school room and as he got to the door I saw this horrid big rabbit suddenly appear from nowhere, grab the lunch bag from his little hand, and make off with it in a flash!"

Well, Norman's lessons are sometimes obscure, his methods unconventional, but it can fairly be said that no one whose life he touches is ever quite the same again. Maybe this can be clarified by giving an in-depth example. Let's take Harry the telephone repairman for instance.

Harry's life assumed its definitive form when he was ten years old. That was the year he fixed his mother's vacuum cleaner. Up to that point he hadn't been much use to anybody, and this was the first time Harry was "appreciated." He liked it. He liked it so much that from then on he went around fixing everything for everybody. Radios, television sets, household appliances, automobiles. Harry made plenty of friends as the years rolled by. Good old Harry! Eventually he even got his wife that way. Friends of his parents had this poorly constructed washing-machine and this well-constructed daughter. Harry took care of both.

Twenty years away from his mother's vacuum cleaner Harry had found the perfect niche. He fixed people's telephones, and the phone company paid him for it. He was so good at it that for a long time they kept him downtown in the business district. He liked the challenges and he liked the fixing, but he sure missed the appreciation. But then he was transferred uptown—apartments and small businesses. Harry was looking forward to being loved again.

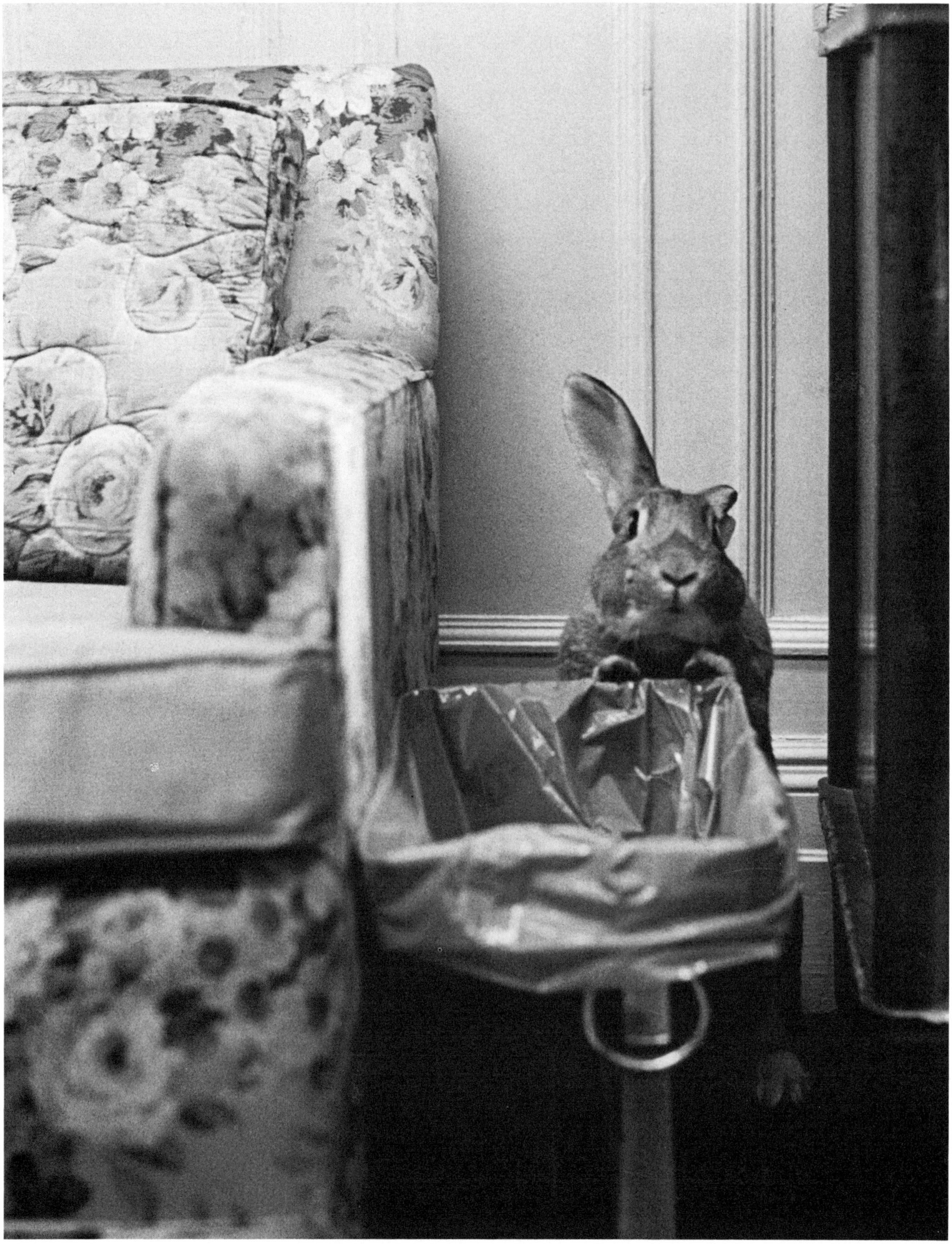

Today, for instance, he was sent to a nursery school with a cutesy name like they all have. The dispatcher gave him a funny look as he handed him the address. Harry asked, "Whassa' matter?"

"Nothin'," the dispatcher said. "The lady there is very pretty and very nice. You'll like it."

Harry was sure he'd like it. This pretty lady was going to be all agitated and fluttery because the school phone didn't work and he'd fix it and she'd be admiring and warm and grateful. She might even call all the little kids in to watch the repairman do his magic. Well, he'd explain to them as best he could, in terms suitable to their age.

As Harry was rehearsing his speech to the children he came to the address: a big, beautiful old church with a garden. He had a twinge of disappointment—something to do with the idea that the pretty lady might be a nun. He had no time to follow that up because he had to ask directions and find the office. There was no problem about finding the school; he wasn't deaf. He hadn't expected so *many* children—maybe they'd have to watch him in small groups, five minutes for each before the next group's turn.

He knocked on the office door and walked in. I doubt if anyone could notice the faint flourish in his entrance. No little kids in the room. No agitated pretty lady. Just a skinny fourteen-year-old girl with long red hair and freckles. He'd have to make do with this kid until the teacher came. He smiled at the kid charmingly and asked, "You the boss of this school?"

She didn't smile back. "I'm a teacher's aide."

"I came to fix the phone," he announced. "I c'n tell."

The kid's stony-faced monotone made Harry a little uneasy. He liked people to *respond*. "Where is it?"

"Right in front of you."

Somehow this damn kid was making him feel awkward. This was *his* game and he was supposed to be master of the situation. Yeah, there was the phone on the desk next to the sofa. He picked up the receiver and deliberately turned away from the kid's impassive stare. Dead. He tugged the cord and heard a loose end scratch on the floor behind the couch. He walked over to the other side of the couch and saw the other broken end.

He turned to the kid. "Is the teacher coming back soon?"

"No."

"Do you think some of the little kids might like to see me put this wire back together?"

"No."

Harry flushed. He didn't know what this kid was doing to him but he sure didn't like it. He spliced the two ends of the wire speedily and expertly. He dropped the repaired wire behind the couch and picked up the receiver. Dead—dead? Couldn't be! Dead!

He pulled the newly spliced cord and out it came from behind the couch, severed, just like the first time. He looked at it. He slowly turned to the girl. She was staring at him with that same poker-face. "Did you see me just splice this wire?"

"What's 'splice'?"

"Put it together. Repair it."

"No."

Before he could sort himself out he heard a shrill voice from the doorway behind him:

"We saw you put the wire together, mister."

Still dazedly holding the loose wire, Harry turned slowly and saw three little kids in the doorway. They were three, maybe four years old. Nice kids—with expressions on their faces.

"Did you come to watch me fix the phone?"

"No. We came to see Norman."

"My name is Harry. Who's Norman?"

"Norman is our rabbit. He goes behind the couch and he eats telephone wires in one bite. Are you new? We thought we knew all the telephone men."

The dispatcher's face flashed before Harry's eyes. He hadn't really yet gotten it all together, but he reached over and pulled the couch away from the wall. There was a rabbit. There was, in fact, the biggest, fattest rabbit Harry had ever seen. It wasn't at all afraid of him. It came up to his leg, sniffed, and stood up on its hind legs as if begging.

"He wants you to give him wire to chew. All the telephone men give him wire. They sent him a basket of wire for Christmas."

Harry sat down on the couch. He looked at the little kids but they had lost interest in him completely. They were playing with Norman, who had also lost interest in him. He looked at the red-headed girl. Her gaze was as steady, empty, and relentless as ever. He spliced the wire again. This time his hands were trembling a little. He tacked the wire up high, picked up the receiver, and called to report in. As the clerk went down the list of questions on the form, Harry's spirits picked up a bit. He'd thought of a way he could restore himself a little.

"Cause?" asked the clerk.

"Rabbit," said Harry expectantly.

"Yeah," said the clerk.

Gretchen, the pretty lady who runs the school, is not agitated by ailing telephones, wailing mothers, or anything else Norman brings about. The only thing she will admit about Norman is that Norman can do no wrong. And she is sufficiently bright, sincere, and articulate to convince anybody that anything Norman does is ultimately constructive and evidence of his superiority.

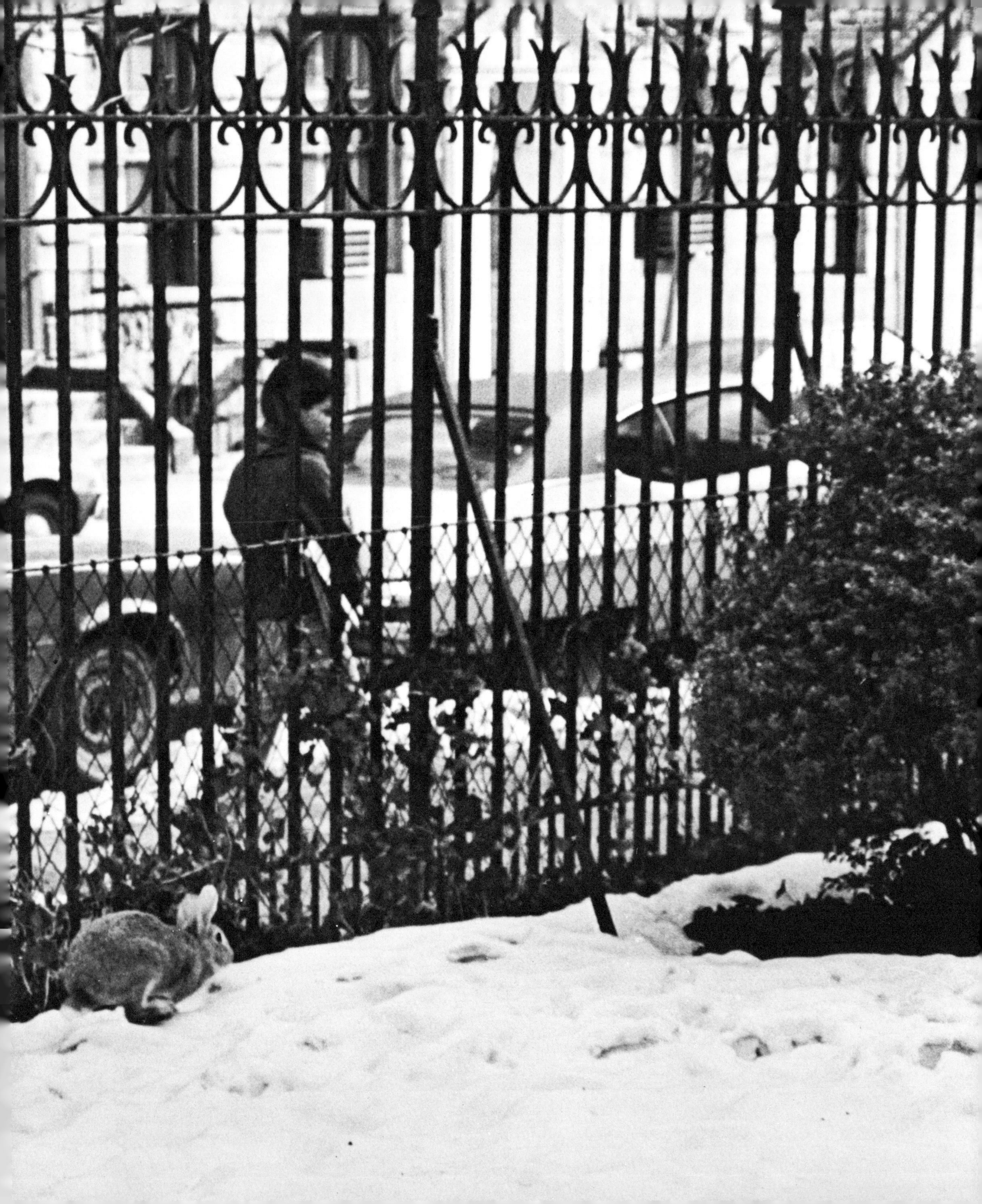

which occupies an entire floor of a large building. And at any given time he may be living with and running free with about forty uninhibited children between the ages of two and six. So he couldn't very well be afraid of people, noise, or rough handling. Afraid? He loves it!

It's also clear that Norman is curious. If a new person appears on the scene, Norman rushes over to check him or her out. Any package draws his interest. When the children group or regroup for an activity, Norman appears promptly in their midst. Since the nursery school always has people coming and going, lots of packages of various kinds, and ever-changing activities, Norman seems like the busiest rabbit there is. You can see that he's always curious.

He's always hungry, too. It quickly becomes apparent why he's so big and fat. Of course, there's regular rabbit food around—vegetables and pellets and such. But nursery schools invariably have cookies, and kids al-

Norman follows on command . . .

. . . and is thoroughly pan-trained.

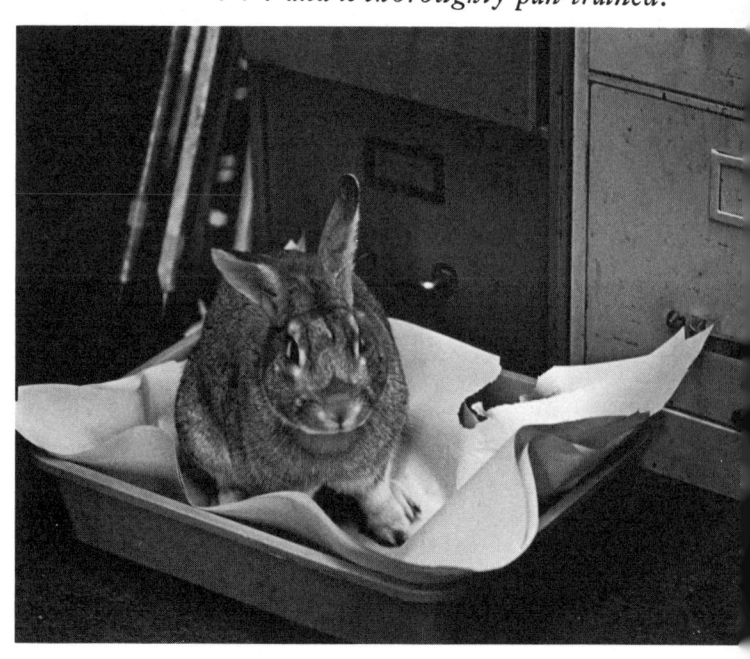

When she was interviewed, Gretchen assumed an attitude of scientific objectivity designed to disarm: "Of course, I haven't known many rabbits. Only three, really. But of those three there's no question that Norman is by far the most intelligent. There probably are other rabbits equally or more intelligent, but I haven't known any. And I don't know anyone who has known any. All rabbits, as far as I know are dumb bunnies. Norman is a smart bunny. And very squishy."

It is clear that Norman is no timid rabbit. He lives in and has free run of the school,

ways have snacks and lunches. Everybody gives Norman handouts because he's so eager. You'd think that by lunch time he'd be gorged. Then why does he steal the kids' lunch bags? If a child is trying to unwrap a lunch package, Norman will push his hands away and press to get at it first. It looks as though he's starved, but Gretchen says that he's discriminating and knows which kids to go to. He knows from experience whose mothers give them what, and just to make sure, he checks them out with a sniff as they arrive at school.

Norman often appears aggressive. One doesn't think of bunnies as aggressive animals. Of course, he doesn't bite or scratch but he grabs, he pushes people's hands away from their food, he squeezes himself in when groups are forming. That's it—it's not so much that he's aggressive, he's *pushy*.

All of this is easy to see. Norman is unafraid, curious, hungry, and pushy. Does that mean he's intelligent? Gretchen would say it does. She'd ask if you could adapt as well as Norman to living in a nursery school. (You couldn't.) If you objected on the grounds that adaptability is different from intelligence, you would get a dissertation on the imperfections of the concept "intelligence" and a list of Norman's accomplishments in the field of learning. He has learned his name and to come when called, he's learned to follow on command, to sit up and beg, to play dead, and to use the litter pan.

When asked how she had taught Norman all these wonderful things, Gretchen showed a little embarrassment. She hesitated, laughed a self-conscious little laugh, and "admitted" (in a hushed, secret voice) that Norman would do *anything*, absolutely anything, for Oreo cookies. As though there were something degrading about Norman being motivated by anything other than the pure burning flame of scholarship. Oh, Gretchen knows better; she knows about motivation. But there was something about Oreos that dulled the luster of the Norman image.

And that's one of the most interesting things about this most interesting rabbit. He

He also plays dead.

has an image, an aura, a mystique. The children deal with him as one of themselves, a favored one. Each of them speaks of him as "my Norman," and so does Gretchen. Other adults in the school (teachers, teachers' aides, student teachers, student nurses, social workers, etc.) talk about "our Norman." Many others are also involved. The school operates in a building of the Episcopal Church of the Holy Trinity. When church personnel began to visit Norman, they talked about him, as do all who meet him. Pretty soon parishioners began stopping by. An assistant priest began speaking of Norman as "our mascot." Pretty soon the rector was heard referring to "our" rabbit. When the bishop was being taken around the church grounds, the very first stop was an introduction to Norman. There are rumors that the diocese has taken a proprietary interest. Total strangers from other parts of town show up at the school to ask if they may see Norman. An organist was seen wearing a T-shirt with a picture of a rabbit on the front and the caption "I love Norman."

This is not a fad. It's been developing slowly but consistently since Gretchen acquired Norman (from the children's section of the Bronx Zoo) about a year and a half ago. These people at the school are not faddists; they are emotionally committed. They take Norman unto themselves ("my Norman," "our Norman"). He is an adornment to their egos. They're proud of him and, by association, they gain stature themselves by virtue of their relationship with him.

It is an important and obvious fact that Norman inspires pride. Everybody wants to show him off to everybody else. When they can't show him, they talk about him: "Well, we have this rabbit and you wouldn't believe—." And it's true—nobody believes. You have to meet him. Then you too fall under his spell.

There seems to be a sort of underground movement to strengthen the sense that there is more to Norman than meets the eye. Gretchen made a joke about his turning into a prince, but she had a slip of the tongue and said "priest." An irreverent wag even referred to Norman as the spirit that invests the church. One day Norman was hopping around and around one of the teachers while she looked adoringly down on him. She raised her head and, with dreamy eyes fixed on infinity, sighed, "I wonder if I can keep the magic circle he's making around me!"

Since Norman is a talisman for an ever-growing community, there are all sorts of fascinating sociological aspects to consider. It's clear, for example, that in some way he confers status. If one were to walk over to a busily conversing group and announce, "I just came from Norman," one would immediately become the center of attention, seize leadership of the group. It was much the same with the king's couriers in ancient times.

A group symbol, such as a national flag, becomes invested with all the high qualities that constitute group pride. When the symbol is a living creature, it becomes adored. High offices are created ("Keeper of the Flag," "Guardian of the Seal," "Monitor of the Rabbit"), and the symbol is used as an instrument for bestowing honor.

One young family was recently privileged in this manner. The mother spent a good bit of time around the church and got quite chummy with Gretchen and Norman. She did, in fact, fall head over heels under the spell. A modest and genteel lady who would never be forward about anything, she found herself one day in Gretchen's office earnestly importuning, "Gretchen, there's no doubt that, for a rabbit, Norman is old enough to have a sleep-over! Of course, Morgan will be upset, but once he meets Norman everything will be fine." (You should know that Morgan, the *pater familias*, would be upset only because he works "downtown." People who work downtown must, if they are responsible

This is Norman's estate.

CHURCH OF THE HOLY TRINITY

THE REV F. REID ISAAC RECTOR
THE REV F.S. BALDWIN CURATE
* FEBRUARY 13, 1977 *
6TH SUNDAY AFTER
EPIPHANY

8:30 AM   EUCHARIST
10:30 AM EUCHARIST
PREACHER
F. REID ISAAC
EVERY WEDNESDAY
6:30 PM   EUCHARIST

These are his private chambers.

Norman sharing a Valentine's Day project with the children.

in their careers, develop a hypersensitivity in matters of convention, propriety, correctness. They may be, as Morgan is, easygoing, good-natured, and broad-minded. But not a hint of these qualities dare drift downtown.)

At any rate, the sleep-over was arranged. The lady was right. Norman was completely at ease and his hostess was in seventh heaven, totally occupied with her guest. As predicted, Morgan's uneasiness was quickly subdued by Norman's charm. Picture the scene on Sunday night, the windup of a perfect weekend:

Morgan is in his study reviewing some "material." His spouse is sitting in the living room, still entranced (I use the word advisedly) by Norman, who is under a table munching contentedly. The telephone rings. Our lady, eyes riveted on Norman, whose every movement fascinates her, absent-mindedly picks up the phone:

"Hello?"

"Hello there. I do hate to bother you at this ungodly hour but I have an urgent question for Morgan. May I disturb him?" (Oh, those smooth, correct, downtown tones!)

"Uh. Oh yes. No bother. He's right here under the table munching alfalfa."

83

Norman sharing lunch with Gretchen.

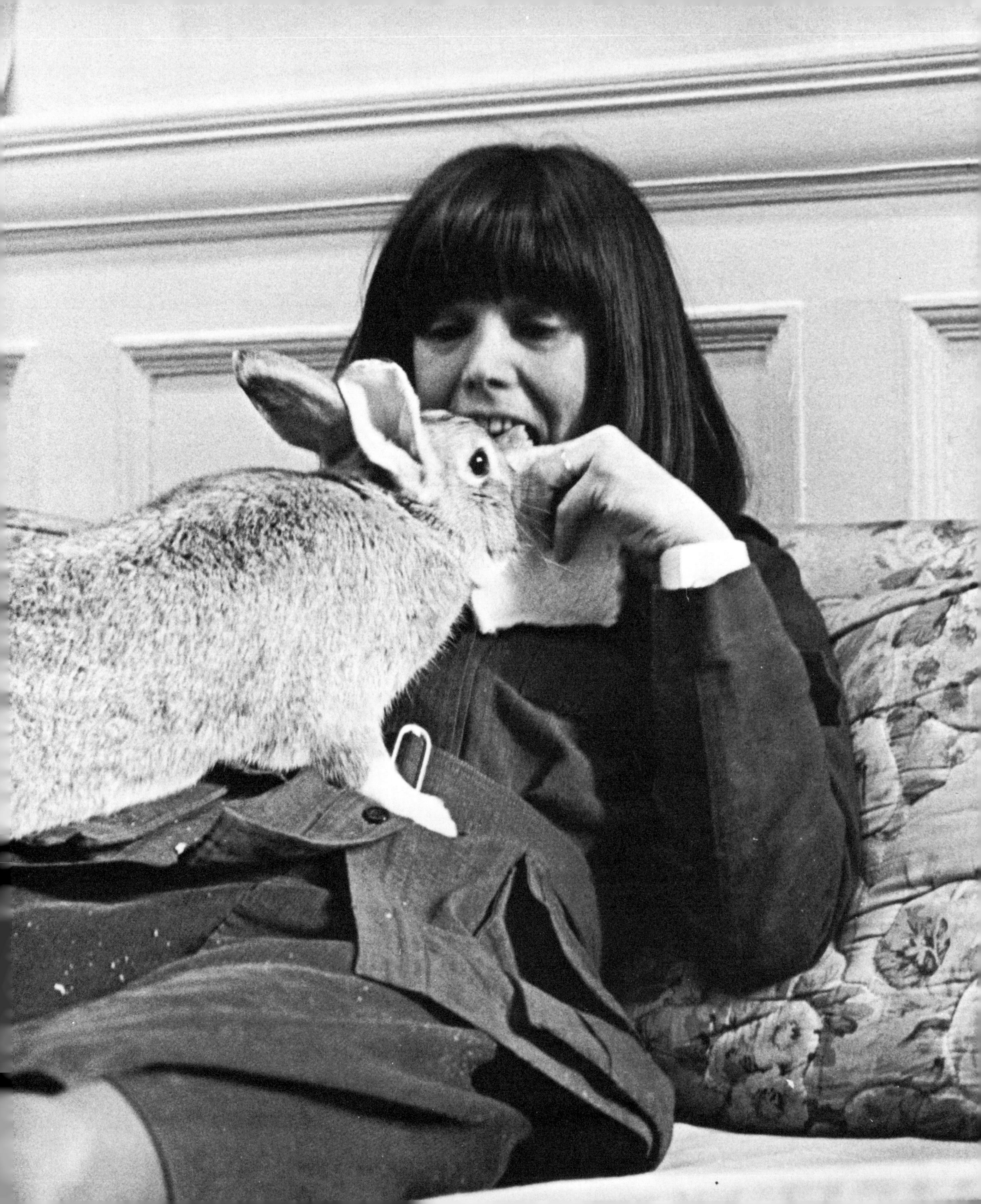

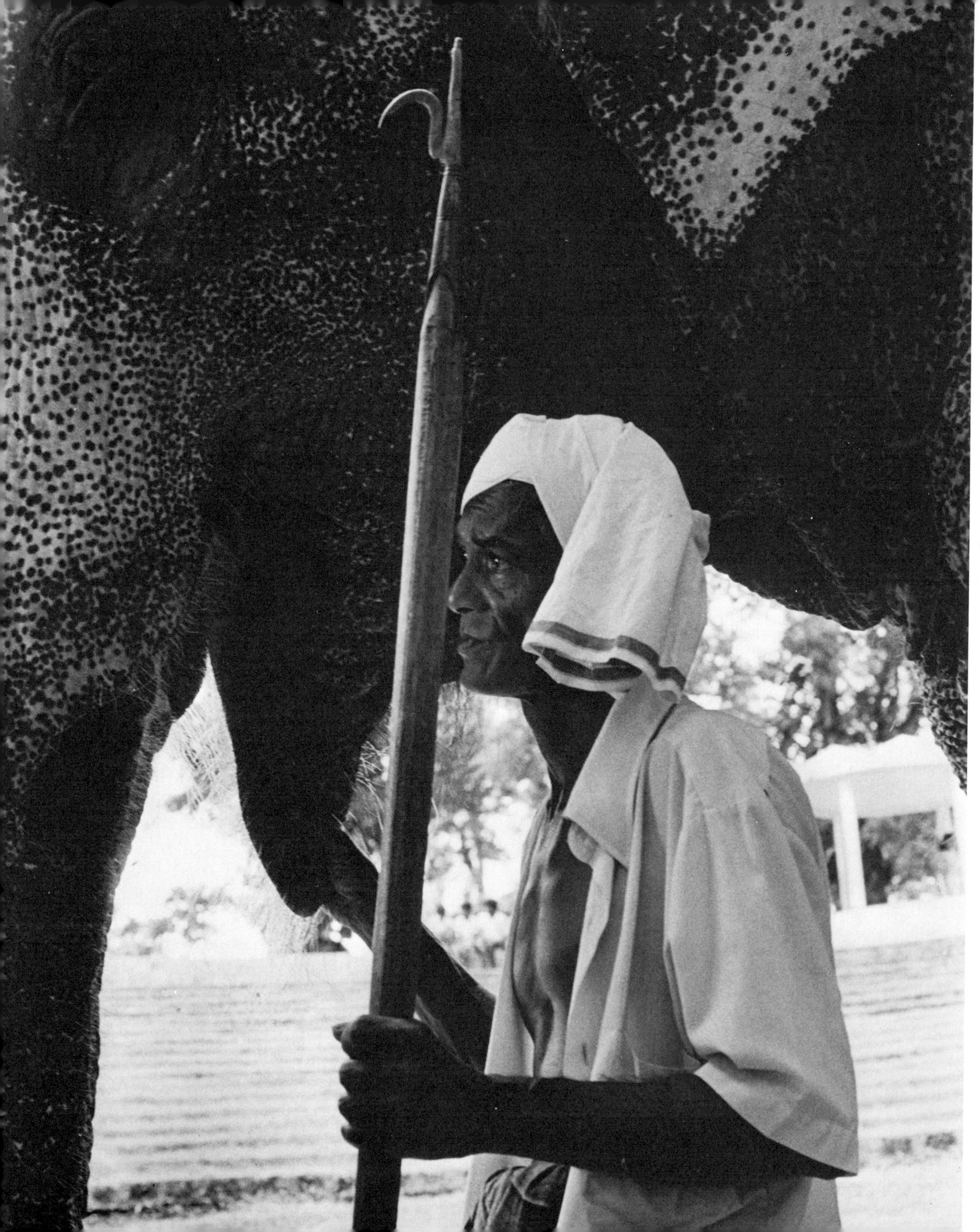

Behold Now Behemoth

I do not mean to call an elephant a vulgar animal; but if you think about him carefully, you will find that his non-vulgarity consists in such gentleness as is possible to elephantine nature; in the way he will lift his foot if a child lies in his way; and in his sensitive trunk, and still more sensitive mind, and in his capability of pique on points of honor.
—JOHN RUSKIN: Modern Painters, *IX*

Dhanipala the mahout and his elephant Ransi had worked hard that morning. Hour after hour they had lifted, hauled, and piled up teak logs in the tropical heat and humidity. "Danny" would have had trouble getting through the morning without the help of a bottle of arrack, the mahout's friend. After work he bathed Ransi, scrubbed her skin with a coconut shell, and then, while she played in the water, he lolled on the bank and emptied his bottle. Not surprisingly, he fell fast asleep. Ransi would have splashed around for hours, but she couldn't go for hours without eating. She has to eat four hundred pounds a day, so food is usually on her mind. So, after a while, she lumbered up the bank and tore down some palm-tree branches, from which she delicately stripped the leaves and a bit of bark and ate them. She walked over and stood stolidly next to the sleeping Danny, gently waving her trunk back and forth.

In a little while she needed another snack. Having taken care of that, she again took up her vigil over Danny. Several hours passed in this fashion. When the light began to fade, Ransi got a little uneasy. She blew air through her trunk so that it came out in a whistling-whooshing sound. She nudged Danny gently with her trunk until he struck out at her in his stupor. Undaunted, she pushed and mauled him until he was as conscious as he could manage to be. He sat up, but that was the best he could do. Ransi circled his chest with her trunk. He thought she was being affectionate, because she often greeted him with a hug, so he reached up and patted her cheek. Instead of letting it go at that, she lifted her trunk so

87

that Danny's legs were dangling a few feet off the ground, headed for the road, and took off for home.

For thousands of years elephants and their mahouts have been working together and taking care of each other on the island of Sri Lanka (formerly Ceylon), where Danny and Ransi live. Plenty of time to form a strong emotional bond. The elephant is an exceptionally large and strong animal with a great deal of intelligence, and—at least equally important—he also has an unusual emotional capacity, which enables him to form complex relationships. This may be because an elephant's early years are lived in a close family structure with a devoted mother. A herd will show great excitement about a newborn elephant, a fuss out of all proportion to the baby's size. At birth the Asian elephant weighs less than two hundred pounds and stands between two and three feet tall. The mothers and aunts are very protective of the youngsters, quick to gather the little ones under their bellies at the slightest disturbance.

Most mahouts are low-salaried workers, descended from a long line of mahouts who have rarely owned the elephants they work with. Each mahout-elephant relationship is shaped by the personalities of the particular

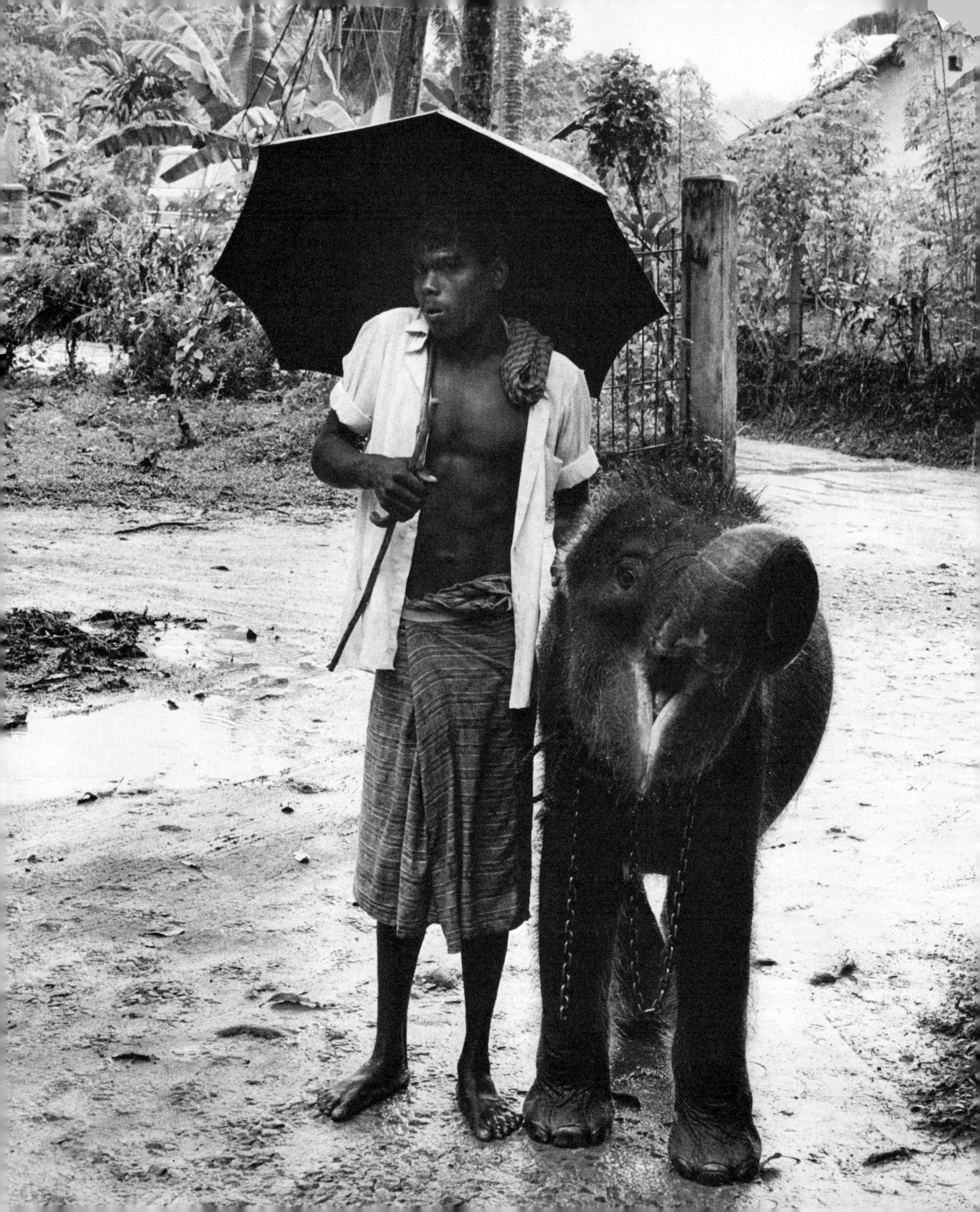

pair. An unfriendly mahout, for example, may have a devoted animal but one that's likely to be unfriendly to other humans. Such an elephant can be dangerous.

Bhandara Dhanipala, whom we're calling Danny, is a nice fellow, and his elephants are nice elephants. They are warm, devoted, and gentle creatures who are aware of their size and strength and are careful of the fragile humans they live and work with. Like many mahouts, Danny grew up with elephants. Unlike many of them, however, he did not accept elephants offhandedly as just another part of the environment—he was fascinated by them. Despite his small size and quiet manner, Danny is "the complete elephant man." His grandfather, father, and older brother have all been elephant trainers. Danny tagged after them from his earliest years and later worked alongside them. The first dream he remembers is one in which he saw himself riding an elephant. The road to his school was frequently crossed by elephants going to work, and since the young Danny followed any elephant that crossed his path, his teachers never even got to know him. It is not surprising that Danny became an outstanding elephant handler and trainer.

On the island of Sri Lanka, Danny, although very much alive and active, is almost a legend. Elephant people tell many stories of his skill and his adventures, like the one about Mina, whom Danny trained and who eventually went to work with another mahout at a sawmill. Because of a mishap with a heavy log, the mahout's arm was broken, and in a rage he whipped out his heavy knife and plunged it into the elephant's body. Maddened by pain and fear, the elephant plunged into the river

The wild elephants usually travel in small, close-knit family groups. This family does not seem concerned about the vacant government rest-house in the background.

and refused to come out, aggressively charging anyone who tried to remove her. Each worker had to withdraw from the panicked animal's frantic attacks, and finally, after three days and many futile efforts, Danny was summoned. The mahouts shook their heads sorrowfully. They knew that Danny would not retire in defeat; his reputation, his pride, his

This ancient stupa, guarded by a wall of carved elephants, attests to the age-old partnership of elephant and man in Sri Lanka.

life work could be sustained only by success or by a heroic death. And they were sure that he couldn't succeed this time. They whispered to each other that the elephant's owners were offering Danny as a sacrifice to the river, hoping that the appeased river would give up the elephant.

Danny stood on the edge of the river and spoke to the elephant. The elephant looked toward the shore, not at Danny in particular but at the crowd that had gathered to watch the drama. The elephant glared at them with hate and fear, and Danny was frightened to have so many eyes riveted on him. He felt that the elephant must share his feelings and so he asked that everybody leave, and the crowd retreated to watch the confrontation from behind bushes and trees.

Alone on the shore, Danny stepped to the water's edge. Instantly the elephant charged him, trying to catch him with her trunk. When Danny jumped back on the shore, the elephant stopped, unwilling to leave the water even to pursue her attack. Danny thought to himself: If I am just a man to her, she will kill me. But if I can get her to recognize me as her old trainer, perhaps she will be calm. He changed from his work clothes into the khaki shirt and shorts he wore as a trainer, and he got a bunch of bananas, his usual reward for the animals he trained. Once again, very tentatively, he approached the water, his outstretched hand offering a banana. Softly he repeated the elephant's name: "Mina, Mina." Again the elephant charged him. At that moment he didn't know if she was coming to him or at him, and it flashed through his mind that thousands of hidden eyes were on him. He was trembling as he said to himself, "This is my life, and I have to do what I have to do." So he stood there and would not retreat. The elephant, starved by three days in the water, took the banana. Danny offered her more bananas, one by one, stepping back a few feet at a time until the elephant was on the shore. They were both very nervous, and half the bananas were gone before the elephant took her eyes off him. But he worked his way behind her and started patting her, edging around her side and calling her name softly as he kept feeding her. Danny recalls that by the time he got so far as to pat her cheek, her panic had receded enough for her to recognize him. The battle was won. Mina followed him to the owner's compound, and they stayed together for three days and three nights while he treated her knife wound and assured himself that she was over her shock.

In Sri Lanka elephants are born free, so

According to an ancient village tradition, a mother who carries her young child under the body of an elephant insures that some of the beast's courage and strength passes into the child.

It is rare to spot a lone male, known as a rogue. One is lucky to see a rogue and even luckier to have a river in between.

If the trappers don't move or make a sound, and if the wind is right, there's very little chance that the elephants will notice them.

before they can be trained they must be captured. Most of the elephants are caught by a traditional method that depends for its effectiveness on the nearsightedness of the animals and the bravery of the men. The elephant men hide in the bush along the elephants' path to a water hole. As long as the wind does not carry the men's scent to the animals, and as long as they remain still, they will be undetected as the herd passes. A trapper emerges when the last elephant passes and slips a rope noose around one of its hind legs. As the leg pulls forward it trips a prearranged counterweight which lifts the leg high so that the elephant

In a surprise move, the elephant suddenly snaps his trunk around, flicking Danny in the shoulder.

As Danny is thrown to the ground unconscious, the trapper in the foreground leaps bravely forward to save him from being stomped upon.

It takes great skill and presence of mind to get a noose around the leg of a wild elephant.

The trappers truss the elephant in a flash. Danny is in the left background.

falls over. In a flash the rest of the crew trusses the other legs and the neck, attaching the ropes to heavy tree trunks. All this must be skillfully and quickly accomplished to avoid injury to the men and to place the ropes so that they do not harm the panicky elephant as he struggles.

The animal may then have to be transported by pulling him with a truck. The trappers hold the ropes taut, front and rear, as the truck slowly drags the animal. Here too the trappers must be alert, for the elephant will quickly seize any opportunity to attack. Once, while holding the front rope, Danny tripped into a pit about two feet deep. Swiftly the ele-

He succeeds in dragging Danny to safety as the elephant sways threateningly from side to side.

After the newly caught elephant has been starved for a few days, he is offered bananas. He isn't quick to make friends, though, and the offer is tentative.

Danny works a great deal by touch.

This elephant has just been taught to lift his foreleg on command . . .

phant was upon him. Danny rolled himself into a ball in the pit, covering his head with his arms. The elephant was afraid to step into the pit but stayed at the edge and began beating Danny with his trunk. Danny lost consciousness. His brother, who was one of the trappers, hit the elephant on a sensitive part of the trunk, and the animal moved away far enough for the other men to drag Danny out of the hole. He was unconscious for about fifteen minutes, and when he came to, spitting blood from the loss of all his teeth, badly bruised, and in severe pain and nervous shock, he thought he was going to die. He was almost sorry when he realized he would not die, because that meant he must haul himself up and, bruised and bleeding, get the elephant to its destination. A trapper who abandoned a hunt could no longer get work with elephants.

You would think that after such hair-raising adventures an elephant man would become afraid, that the odds were bound to catch up with one after many years of working with the mammoth beasts and after so many narrow escapes. Not so with Danny. "I have always lived with elephants and I am willing to die with elephants. It's better to die this way because I love it. I have always given my life to it."

The process of taming consists essentially of encouraging the elephant to overcome his fear of man. In other words, the trainer makes friends with the animal. Once the elephant reaches its destination it is securely trussed and left for a short period without food or water. The trainer then offers the hungry animal sugar cane and sweet fruits. When thirst has built up he offers cool water. He repeats the name he has chosen for the animal and says "Deri" (take) over and over again. At first the elephant approaches the food hesitantly, but he soon learns that at certain times this man will bring him delicious food and refreshing water. As the food is offered, the trainer comes closer and closer. He tries to pat the animal, hoping that the simultaneous offer-

. . . and to open his mouth wide.

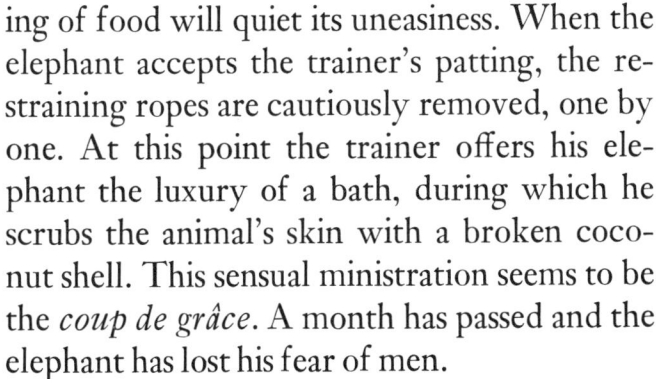

Danny is teaching his son the pressure points and demonstrating the goad, which he rarely uses.

ing of food will quiet its uneasiness. When the elephant accepts the trainer's patting, the restraining ropes are cautiously removed, one by one. At this point the trainer offers his elephant the luxury of a bath, during which he scrubs the animal's skin with a broken coconut shell. This sensual ministration seems to be the *coup de grâce*. A month has passed and the elephant has lost his fear of men.

Now begins the training of the tame elephant. The first command is usually "Bileh" (lift your leg), and as it is given the trainer taps the elephant behind one of the front legs. For this purpose the trainers use a goad, at the tip of which is a metal hook with a dull point. This hook is used to reach and press on various pressure points to signal a desired action.

The elephant is taught to kneel ("Danuh"), and an assistant climbs on his back while the trainer holds his ear. When the animal is accustomed to the man on his back, he is taught the signal to "go" ("Da-ha"). At first the elephant is guided by the trainer on the ground, but eventually the rider will control the elephant with his feet, varying the pressure points to signal a change in speed or direction. The elephant is taught the commands needed for general care such as feeding and bathing, and then the commands appropriate to the work he'll be assigned to do. On the average, he learns one command a week, so that it takes about a year to train an elephant for logging.

The style of training depends, of course, on the trainer. Danny manages to be firm and clear and, at the same time, gentle to the point of being affectionate. He always rewards the animal with food for success, and he seems to communicate a great deal through his hands as well. He usually works with one hand continually caressing the animal's cheek. He uses the goad as sparingly as possible to reach and press the signal points, preferring, when it's practical, to use a hand instead. In this way he establishes a bond of mutual trust and affection as he trains the elephant. Danny says that any

The best elephant pupils are selected for show training at the Deliwela Zoo.

elephant he has tamed and trained (about one hundred and fifty to date) is his good friend, whom he would trust as he would trust his mother, father, and children.

The commands mentioned above are used all over Sri Lanka and are known as "elephant language." The words have no other meanings and no other purpose except that of communicating with elephants. If a trained elephant were to be taken to another country, a year might be necessary to retrain it in the new elephant language.

There is a science and a mystique about the pressure points. Some are considered very dangerous to the animal, so trainers must learn to be quite precise. In getting the animal to raise its leg, for example, the hook must be well placed, because it is said that wrong placement may touch a spot that will paralyze the leg. There is a very dangerous spot over the elephant's eye, and only a skilled and confident mahout will signal an elephant to move backward by pressing the signal point in that area.

Although elephants have a limited range of vocal expressions, they manage to communicate well. A nervous elephant may blow air through his trunk, producing the whistling-whooshing sound. When he is very upset, perhaps to the point of preparing to charge, he will produce a blood-curdling trumpet, loud enough to be heard for miles. Another common sound, coming from deep inside him, is uttered with the mouth closed, a kind of rumbling "B-D-B-D-B-D" that expresses pleasure and affection, something like a cat's purring.

Perhaps more important than the sounds are the facial and bodily expressions, attitudes, and gestures. An affectionate elephant may run to its trainer and hug him with its trunk. A happy elephant has a lively, joyful air and is likely to be very playful. As Danny puts it: "My elephants are like kids in the water." An elephant who has a pain looks like an elephant who has a pain, and he may, for the benefit of his mahout, point with his trunk to the area that hurts. One of Danny's elephants often feels inadequately appreciated. When that happens, she will perform her tasks perfectly but in a brusque, curt manner that clearly conveys her indignation. Danny says that she always makes him feel guilty.

The elephants in Sri Lanka, like the people, seem quick to smile. Although this gives

This elephant is demonstrating remarkable control; and Danny's son, under the elephant, is demonstrating remarkable confidence.

Elephants also play a starring role in festivals.

the animals a pleasant expression, it seems to be more a matter of physiognomy than an indication of mood. Still, one can detect variations that seem to accord with mood.

A whole body of legend has grown over the thousands of years during which the elephant has lived in close association with man, each story attesting to real or fancied qualities with which the animal is invested. From these tales one learns that the elephant has enormous physical power, that he is capable of learning and performing complex tasks, and that he forms deep and lasting emotional relationships with man. These relationships—for man as well as elephant—include qualities such as affection, trust, confidence, respect, loyalty, protectiveness, jealousy, and possessiveness. Since both elephants and men are capable of unreasoning fear and anger, however, each is aware that the other is potentially dangerous.

One day a mahout brought his elephant to market. There he saw a small boy persistently teasing the beast, and when the child ignored his warnings the mahout caught him and spanked him with a palm frond. Several years later another boy teased the elephant beyond the animal's tolerance. The elephant swerved, trumpeted, and charged the boy. The terrified bystanders dared not intervene. As the animal caught the boy with his trunk, they were transfixed with horror, expecting the child to be dashed to the ground and killed. The elephant put the boy gently on the ground, pinned him there with a foot, picked up a palm frond with his trunk, and delivered a good facsimile of the spanking his mahout had administered years before.

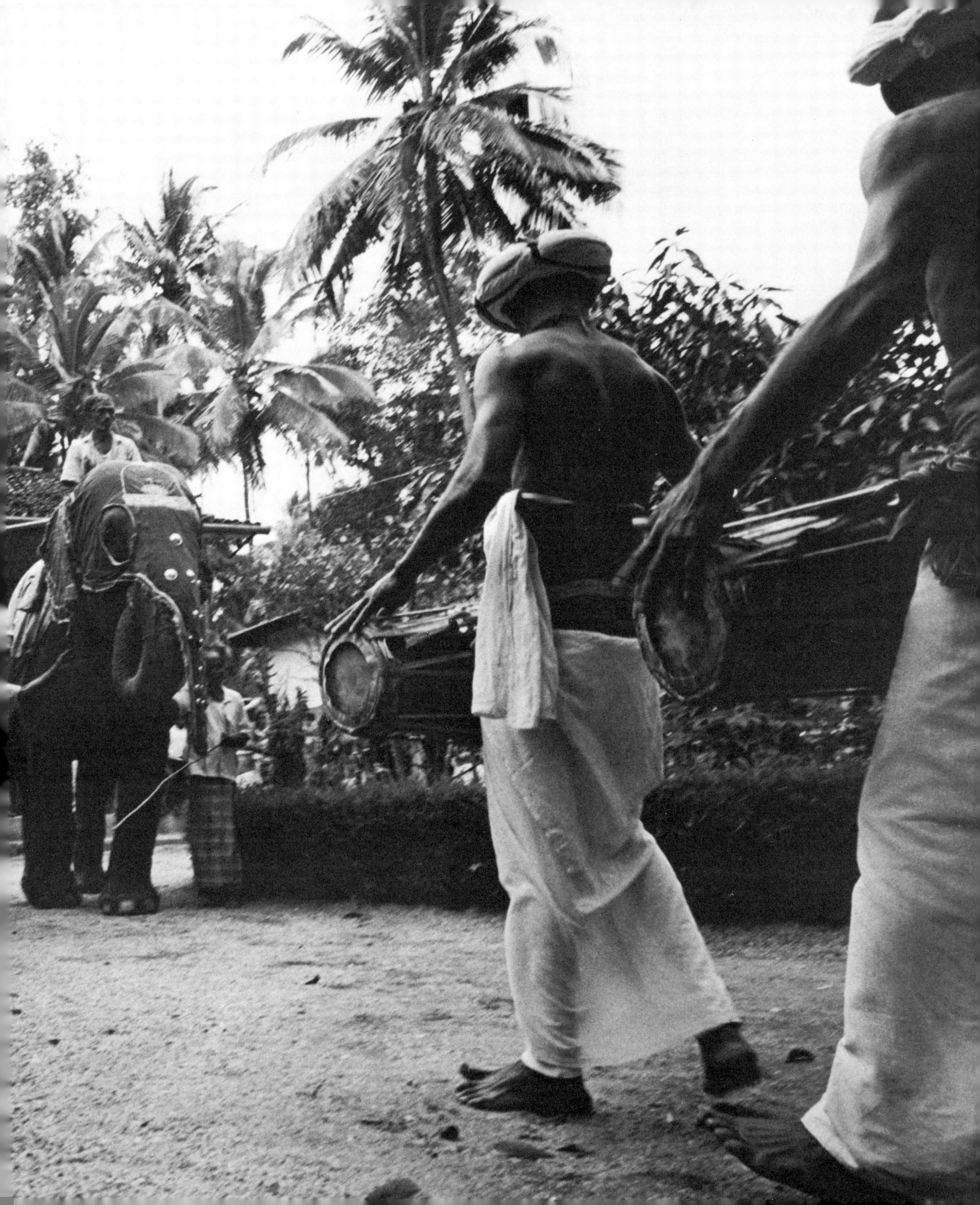

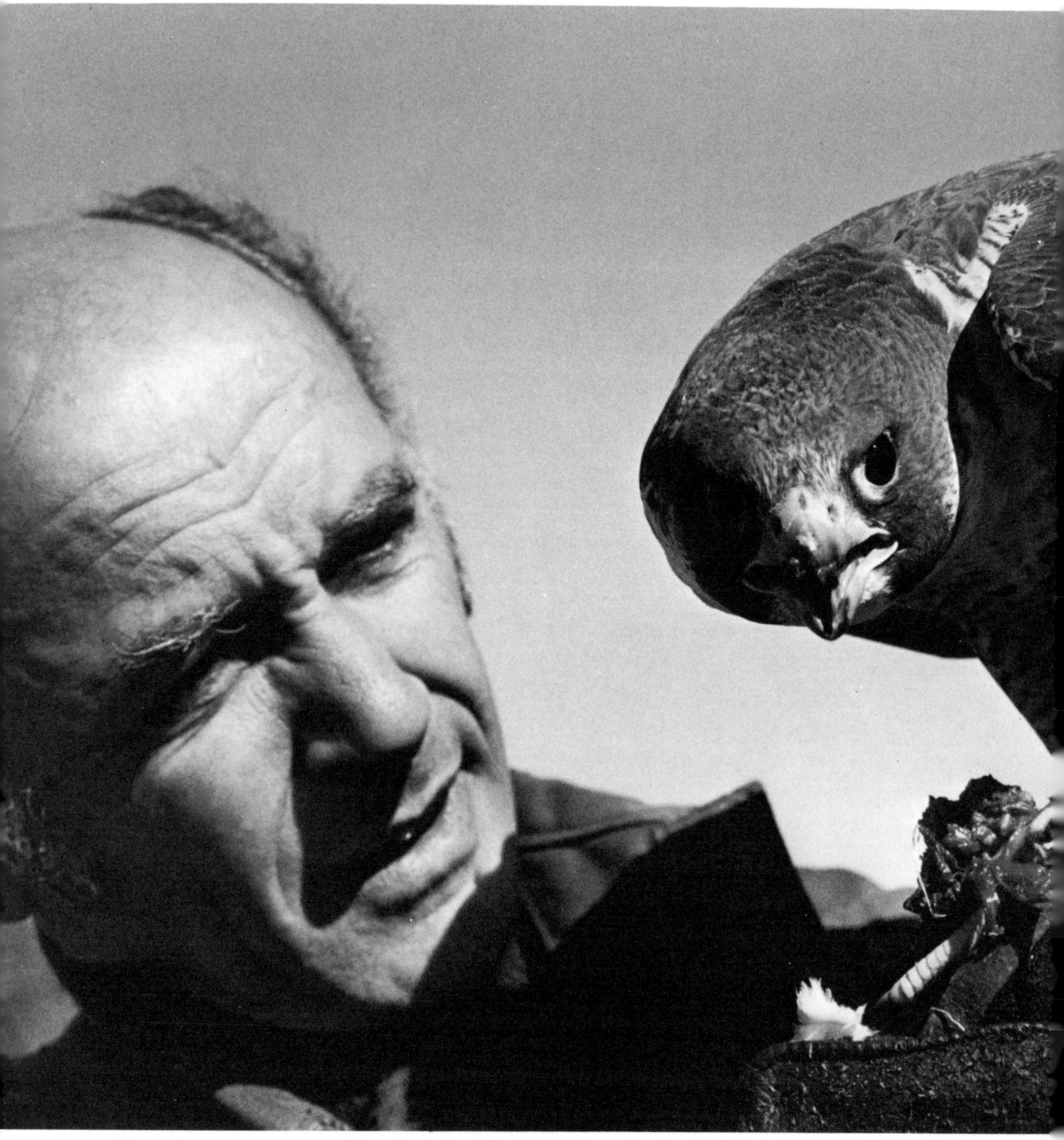

Mayhem in High Places

Birds act by instinct, and ne'er can attain the rectitude of man.
—Mary Lamb,
 The Rook and the Sparrows

Jones Beach is lovely in autumn. The air is exhilarating, and the sea, together with the broad empty reaches of sand, gives a sense of openness and freedom that makes one feel a kinship with the gulls wheeling so gracefully at the water's edge. That's the way Heinz felt as he trudged along, his bare toes digging voluptuously into the yielding sand. He didn't know he felt that way because, like many seventeen-year-olds, Heinz wasn't very articulate about his feelings. On this particular day (October 12, 1941, to be exact—Heinz was exact) his mind was full of butterflies. Monarchs to be exact. They were migrating and there were lots of them. He liked butterflies—not as much as he liked birds but enough to catch them, kill them, mount them, and classify them. His interest was caught by a Buckeye butterfly, a type missing from his collection. He stalked it with the finesse of a born hunter until, when it landed on a goldenrod blossom, it was his. Then as he turned, his eye was caught by some downy feathers in the air, blowing up from behind a large dune, as though someone were shaking a pillow. He started toward the dune, moving cautiously. He didn't know why he was moving cautiously. Maybe it was just habit. But this time, as he reached the dune, his caution was well rewarded. There on the sand in the reed grass was a peregrine falcon fiercely clutching a just-killed marsh hawk.

103

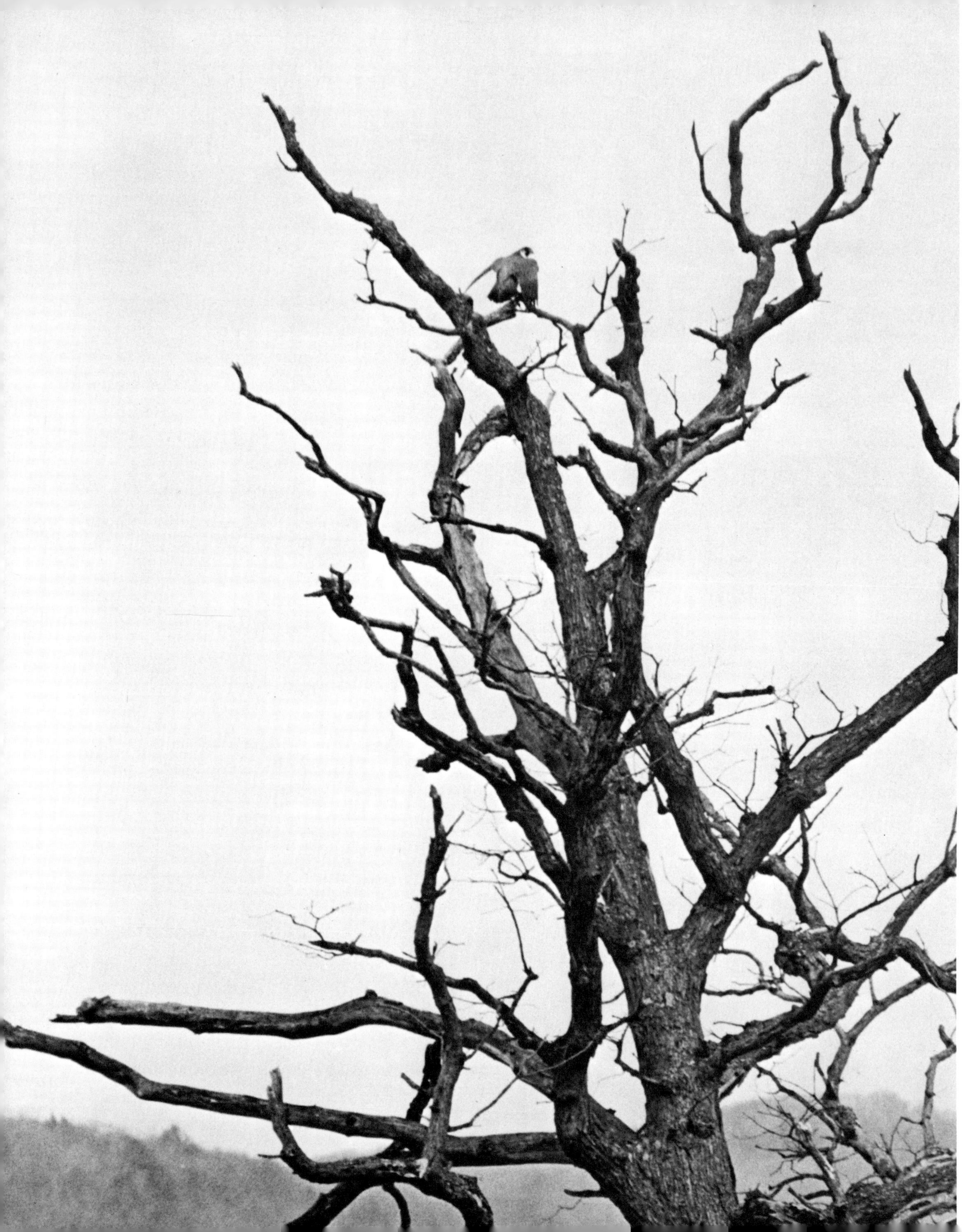

A peregrine falcon is an imposing bird. It's a large, strikingly handsome, no-nonsense animal, and when it's busy tearing apart another large bird it gives one pause. Not Heinz. He ran away fast, but only to deposit the Buckeye he'd captured. He ran back just as fast, then slowly edged up to the falcon, carefully taking off his jacket as he moved. Cautiously he inched ahead, holding the jacket over his head. Heinz had never seen a peregrine before, and the bird, most likely fresh from Greenland, had probably never seen a human. Re-

The rare peregrine falcon can occasionally be spotted during the fall migration.

Careful feeding is basic to the training process. Heinz holds in his mouth part of a wireless transmitter that will help track the gyrfalcon if it gets out of sight.

luctant to leave her prey, she let Heinz get within six feet before she uneasily spread her wings and opened her beak. The motionless Heinz wiggled his toe to draw her gaze downward and, at that instant, he leaped forward and enveloped the bird in his jacket.

I've known a great many seventeen-year-old kids from Long Island, and I just can't picture any of them doing that. For one thing, the ones I've known were all clumpers. None of them had that cautious gait. A few of them were collectors but they tended to collect inanimate things. Some of them occasionally took things they wanted, but just taking things wasn't their passion. Any one of them would have been fascinated by the sudden confrontation with a falcon on her kill. So would you and I. But it's a rare seventeen-year-old whose chief reaction would be to capture it, and a much rarer one would be able to do it. Would you have thought to wiggle your toe?

Obviously, Heinz was different. Even when he was a little boy he was fascinated by birds. He drew pictures of birds at an age when my kids were drawing houses and trees and Mommy and Daddy. The first birds he captured were those he snatched from the pages of magazines. By the time he was seventeen he knew he was going to be an ornithologist. But I don't believe he kidnaped that bird on Jones Beach because of any scientific interest. I think he took it because he wanted to train it, to master it, to hunt other birds with it, and, most of all, just to *have* it. He got someone to show him some things about training falcons, and he did pretty well in training his bird. But it got away eventually.

The hood must be presented carefully and precisely.

Since that time Heinz has become an ornithologist, a college professor. And since that time he's trapped innumerable falcons. I strongly suspect that after that first one the only ones that got away were those he deliberately freed. As an outstanding sport falconer, he has captured, trained, and hunted with many falcons. As an outstanding ornithologist, he was one of the founders of the current efforts to breed American peregrines and restore them to the wild. The right hand giveth while the left hand taketh away.

Peregrines no longer live and breed in the United States. There may be some insig-

Heinz clips the jesses to his gauntlet, while holding the hood in his mouth.

Every motion requires finesse.

nificant exceptions in the far west, but to all intents and purposes the American peregrine was killed off by DDT. Now Heinz Meng, along with a group of scientists, is trying to breed, restore to the wild, and reestablish falcons in the United States. Since the success of that effort depends on an intimate knowledge of falcons, Heinz maintains that falconers are the falcon's best friend.

There's a coordinated breeding program now, and there are strict protective laws. The North American Falconers Association has about four hundred members, each of whom had to convince the organization of his seriousness before admission. Because of the restrictions, not many of them fly peregrines, but a number of closely related birds of prey are available.

The sport of falconry has an ancient tradition in many parts of the world. It was practiced in China over four millennia ago. In western civilization the high point of the sport occurred in the Middle Ages, when it was extremely popular and highly ritualized. Today small, dedicated bands of hunters maintain the practice. And dedication is surely required. It's not easy to get birds, it's very difficult to train them properly, and it's tricky to fly them.

Training the birds is simple to explain but the process is replete with subtleties in its execution. Manuals have been written in every period and in many languages, but personal guidance is important and, in the end, personal experience is the key factor. One basic ele-

Voilà!

107

ment in the whole process is feeding—or rather, not feeding. If you get a falcon hungry enough, he will do things for food that he might otherwise be most reluctant to do. This is much more complex than it sounds, because you must, at the same time, keep him in perfect condition.

The initial problem is to accustom the bird to your presence. Then you must get him to come to your wrist for food. He must also become accustomed to the paraphernalia of the sport—hood, jesses (leg straps), lures, etc. When the bird will accept the wrist, the hood, and the jesses, he is taught to fly to the lure, which is a bird-shaped dummy baited with food and swung around the falconer's head at the end of a long line. The falcon, at first secured by a very long nylon line with a heavy stick on its end (a "creance"), is released and, if it is to eat, it must seize the bait

This bird was carried in a box instead of being hooded. The transmitter wire is attached once the bird is removed from the box.

The falcon is released from the wrist.

on the lure. This is a fundamental exercise because later on, when the falcon flies free, the falconer retrieves it by calling to it and swinging the lure to attract it back. You can see that a lot depends on the bird's being hungry. It may take roughly three to six weeks to train a wild falcon to the point where it can reliably be flown free. Heinz, who is an outstanding expert, has done it in ten days.

The basic practice of falconry is to release the bird, flush the game, and retrieve the falcon and game when the kill has been made. The sequence may vary in that the falcon may be released from the fist after prey is sighted. Lure-flying is, in itself, an exacting and graceful sport, since the falconer can swing his lure in such a manner as to avoid or accede to his falcon's passes. The two, bird and man, can evolve a delicate choreography.

It is indeed dramatic to see a peregrine falcon circle high in the sky and then suddenly plummet down at incredible speed to seize its prey. But for me the greatest excitement is in the aesthetic element. A great falconer such as Heinz knows falcons so well, and understands his own birds so thoroughly, that he works with precision. He and the bird respond to every move, sometimes seeming to anticipate each other. Everything is sure and smooth and graceful. The moment bird and man come together, one senses the presence of a great team. Heinz releases the bird with a small gesture which the falcon completes in its rise. Then, as the bird embellishes the initial thrust,

The falcon flies low to pass at the lure.

wheeling and swooping its variations, Heinz pivots with the circling of the bird and starts the rhythmic swing of the lure. Heinz is moving, the lure is reaching out in delicately controlled swoops, and the falcon coordinates its swerve to make a pass at the lure. Just as the strike is about to be made, Heinz eases into a small dip, the lure dips broadly with him, and the falcon counterpoints by swinging back up into the air and circling for another strike. There are endless variations and it is an endlessly beautiful game.

Flying the falcons after prey is not, to me, a game. For the falconer it's sport, for the falcon it's food, for the prey it's the end. I have seen prey escape, but falcons are animals of deadly efficiency. The basic fact is that the falcon, like man, is a predator. It kills other animals and eats them. The falconer injects himself into that cycle and controls it in a formal manner.

The falconer, despite the nobility, history, and glamour of his tradition, must answer for the destruction of life. His answer may be a disdainful shrug or a disclaimer of responsibility for the so-called "cruelty" of nature. It is, however, a fact that falconry is an act of man and not of nature. And it's the falconer who gets the felled prey. So the issues become those of any form of sport hunting. People hold forth heatedly and vociferously on both sides of this issue. One hears moral arguments and logical arguments. It is my present belief that all the arguments are secondary to the strong emotions of the protagonists. I believe that killing serves powerful emotional needs in some people and that it conflicts with powerful emotional forces in other people. One finds oneself on the side of the fence dictated by his or her emotional constitution and one then finds moral, logical, or any other grounds he can to support his position.

Heinz spoke to me with such enthusiasm about his work and his birds that I asked if he got attached to the birds or felt any affection for them. After a brief pause, he assured me that his birds got the very best of care. I felt as if I had been caught trying to "trap" him into being sentimental. Heinz's response wasn't simply that of the dispassionate scientist. He is, and has been since childhood, a sportsman —one who takes pride in his skill in killing animals by a variety of ritually restricted means.

(He showed me, for example, a number of hunting bows. I couldn't even bend one of them. Maybe if I had been brought up differently I would have learned to delight and take pride in the same things that Heinz does. At any rate, he sure is good at them.)

Nevertheless, the fact is that his birds seem to like him. They welcomed his approach with what can only be described as murmurs of delight. It was clearly distinguishable from the raucous warnings they gave when I got too close. The birds were on low perches to which their jesses were clipped. The perches were just high enough so that the bird could get on and off readily without injury. If the perch were any higher and a bird took off too vigorously, its short jesses would jerk it back and it might be left hanging helplessly upside down. Birds who are unaccustomed to the wrist often find themselves in that predicament, although it happens rarely with experienced falconers. When the bird is transferred from the perch to the wrist, or vice versa, one jess at a time is unclipped from the source and transferred to the destination. You must plan everything and you must be careful.

When the falcons are transported, they are usually hooded, because they're high-strung creatures and the less they see, the less upset they will be. Birds bred in captivity tend to be somewhat less tense than wild ones and have very little fear of man, but captured birds, however well trained, are never really relaxed.

Taming a wild bird calls for the utmost sensitivity to the bird's tensions. The taming starts in darkness, since the birds tend to be calmer when they cannot see well. Most birds are hooded as soon as they are caught, and are kept that way until after the falconer has hand-fed them the first time (usually the second day). During the next feeding, in very dim light, the falconer removes the hood. For the next few days the hood is on only during daylight hours. After the bird is accustomed to finding its food on the falconer's gloved hand, the hand is presented from gradually increasing distances so that the bird learns to "fly to the fist." After about a week, the bird is brought outdoors and set on a block perch with a pan of water nearby. Getting the bird to accept this new circumstance may take one day or many, and, as usual, the falconer is guided by close attention to the bird's reactions. It is no longer considered necessary, or even useful, to spend an inordinate amount of time accustoming the bird to the presence of the falconer ("manning" the falcon). Keen sensitivity to the bird, calm assurance, patience, and clarity of purpose cut the necessary time to ten days or less.

When the falcon is manned, it is then trained to fly to the lure. First it learns to come to the lure for food. Both the falcon and the lure are set up in such a manner as to discourage the bird from just taking off with the lure. This is done by weighting the lure and attaching a creance to the falcon. Gradually the distance is increased, the weight is removed from the lure, and the food is removed from the lure. The falcon learns that if it takes the lure, the falconer will feed it from his fist. Eventually the falcon learns to relinquish its prey in favor of the food the falconer will offer.

When the falcon has learned the sequence well, it can be started on free flight. Naturally, the bird is started when it is hun-

A split second before the lure is seized.

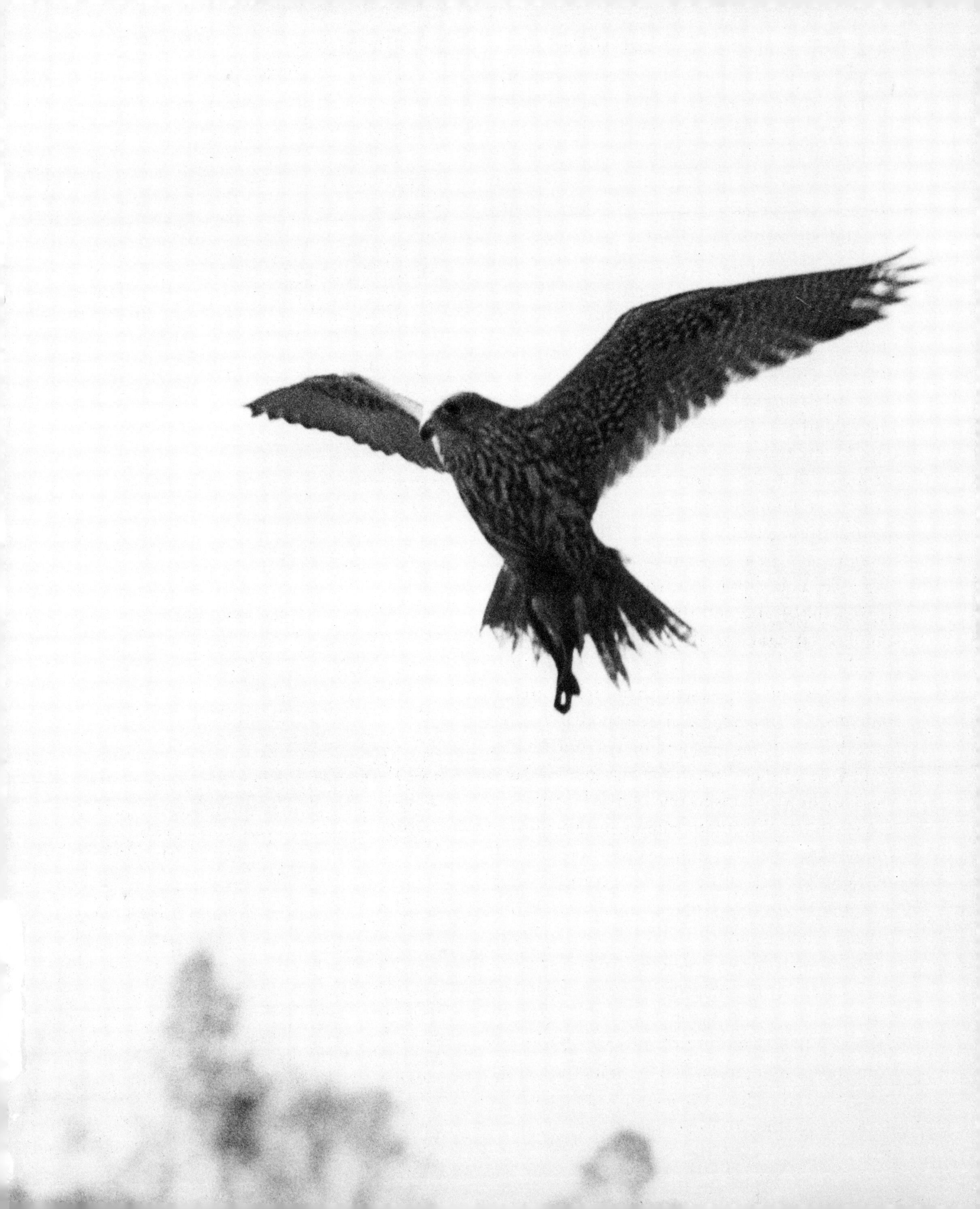

gry. And again it's a gradual process of increasing the difficulty and prolonging the flights. At first the lure is fairly accessible, on the ground. Then it is pulled away and, finally, it is swung in the air. Then follow a series of exercises in which the falcon is made to miss and return, to take the lure on the ground, or to grab it ("bind to" the lure) in mid air. Peregrines are often taught to climb up into the air (called "ringing up" because of the spiral flight pattern) and to circle high in the sky ("waiting on") before being shown the lure and starting their exercises.

After about ten days of this lure training, the falcon is ready for live quarry, for hunting. Heinz trains his birds to be specialists. He decides what the falcon will hunt, dresses its lures to resemble the selected quarry, and limits its hunting to that species. He feels that if the falcon's first exposure is to pigeons, for example, you should not send it after a duck. If you do so you run the risk of its deserting the duck to take off after any stray pigeon in the distance.

I got the impression that Heinz prefers pigeons, for the practical reason that he flies his falcons a great deal and he needs a reliable source of quarry birds. He maintains a large flock of live pigeons to release for hunting exercise and for regular feeding. I also got the impression that he didn't favor crows (although he did show me a carefully constructed crow lure). The problem with crows is that when attacked by a falcon they fight back, which shows a shocking disrespect for the ancient and noble tradition of falconry. Crows also tend to gang up on an attacking falcon, and the picture of an aristocratic falcon gathering up its ruffled feathers for a hasty retreat—well, I've never seen it in any of those antique sporting woodcuts.

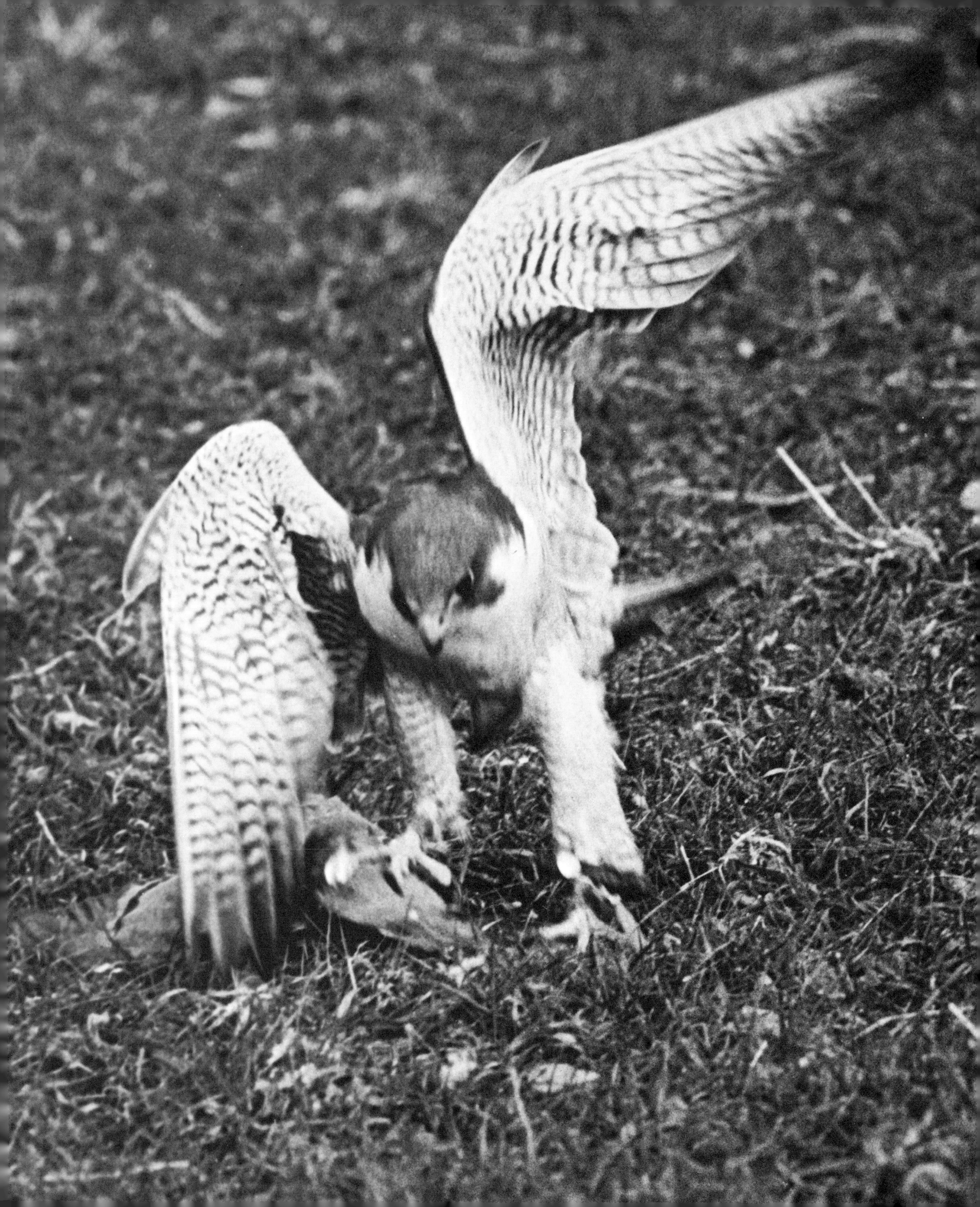

Whereas Heinz Meng is very serious about falcons and falconry, he is too experienced, knowledgeable, and self-assured to be heavy about it. He has, in fact, quite a sense of humor. He told me about a woman who was upset to see him break the neck of a live pigeon. He explained that he killed his pigeons instantly, but the woman accused him of un-Christian behavior. Heinz said that he pointed out to her that the decision about the falcon's diet rested with God and not with himself. Had God decreed that falcons should eat dog food out of cans, he, Heinz, would gladly go along with that.

Heinz does, as a matter of fact, react to people who respond emotionally to the sight of him snapping pigeons' necks. I was present on one occasion when a visitor who came to see the falcons fly was totally unprepared to see Heinz pull a live pigeon from his sack, snap its neck, and pull it apart. She was momentarily stunned, turned green, and walked a short distance away. She was embarrassed by her own behavior and mumbled some excuses, but Heinz, perhaps in deference to her embarrassment, affected not to notice. But he did notice. How do I know? Because his sense of humor betrayed him.

When we returned to Heinz's home he introduced us to a gorgeous great-horned owl. Our lady of the story petted the owl, obviously attracted to the amiable bird. Then she asked, as a sort of doleful afterthought, "Does he hunt, too?" Heinz assured the lady that the owl did indeed hunt. Deer, as a matter of fact. The owl, Heinz offered, has a special fondness for deer eyes, which he swoops down on and pecks out.

The woman recoiled, but Heinz insisted on taking us forthwith to his basement to show us the deer that he and the owl had just killed. He wanted, too, to show us the owl's twin brother who lived in the basement. We saw the deer, or at any rate its skin stretched out on the floor near the hunting bows (with which Heinz apparently assists his owl). He then brought forth an enormous box, like a small dog house, reached in, and drew forth another beautiful great-horned owl on a perch. The beauty of the bird was a welcome sight in those somewhat macabre surroundings, and the woman's face showed her relief as she started to exclaim about the bird. But just as she opened her mouth, Heinz, with the perfect timing of the professional sportsman, pushed the base of the perch and the owl's head leaped up in the air separated from its body.

Of course it was a stuffed owl, which Heinz had been manipulating with consummate artistry. Just as he'd been manipulating the lady. And, come to think of it, just as he manipulates his falcons. Although I'm sure that Heinz sees himself as a scientist and a sportsman, I see him primarily as an artist.

By way of contrast, this falcon and dog belong to an Arab on the Cap Bon peninsula in Tunisia. He's not a glamorous oil sheik in flowing burnoose, but a poverty-stricken Berber who lives in a grass shack. He relies on his dog and his bird to help him get food, since his pitiful earnings don't provide enough.

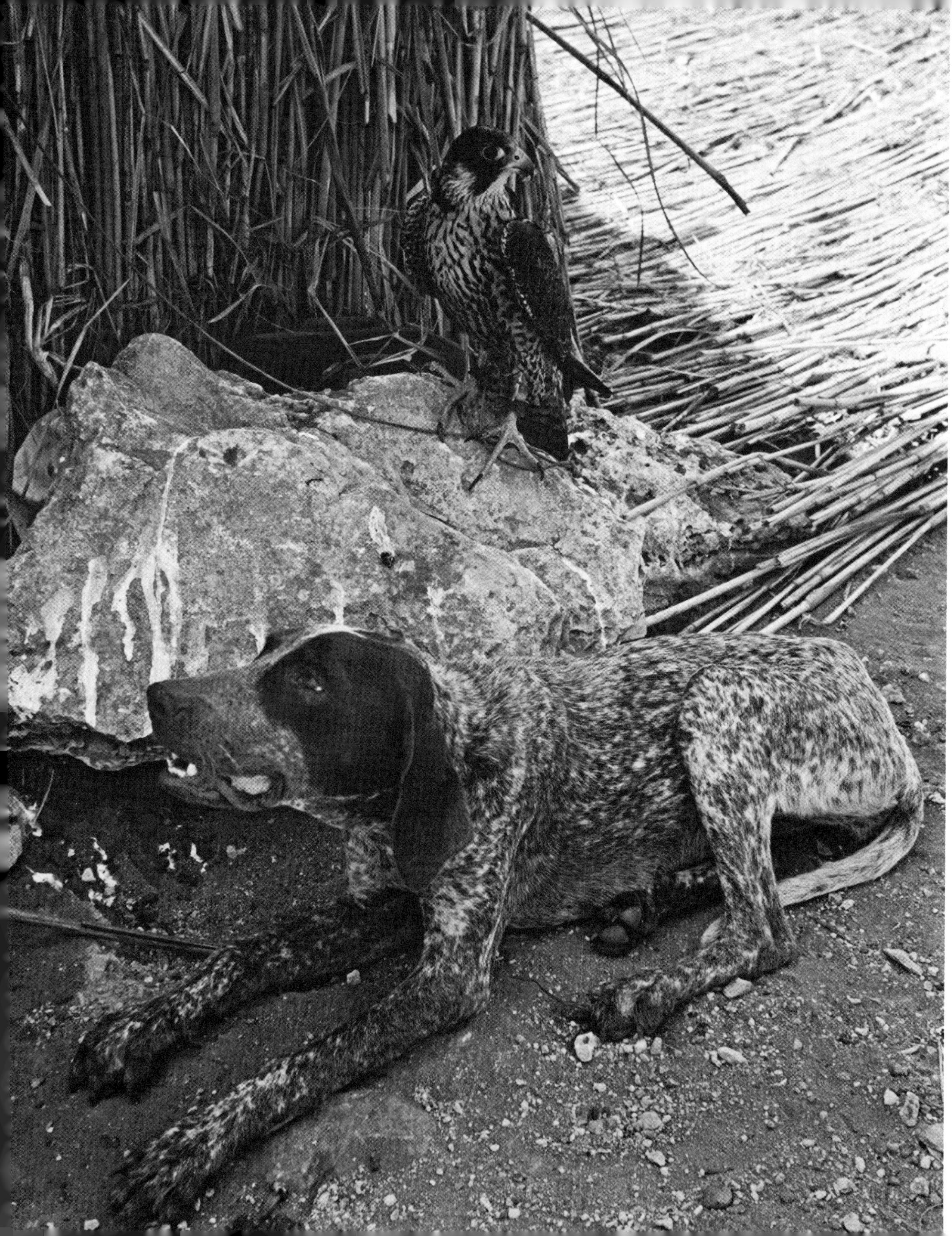

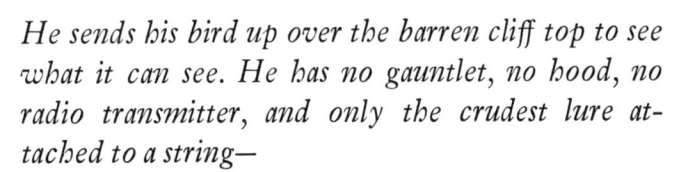

He sends his bird up over the barren cliff top to see what it can see. He has no gauntlet, no hood, no radio transmitter, and only the crudest lure attached to a string—

—but high above the sea, on the bleak, lonely moor, man and bird choreograph a primitive dance.

Sometimes the bird heads toward the sea, as if drawn to the cliff face where it was born . . .

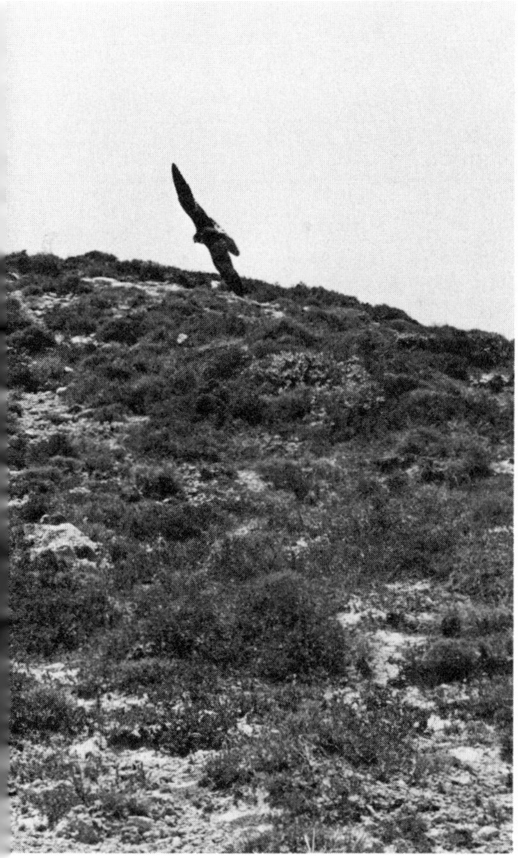

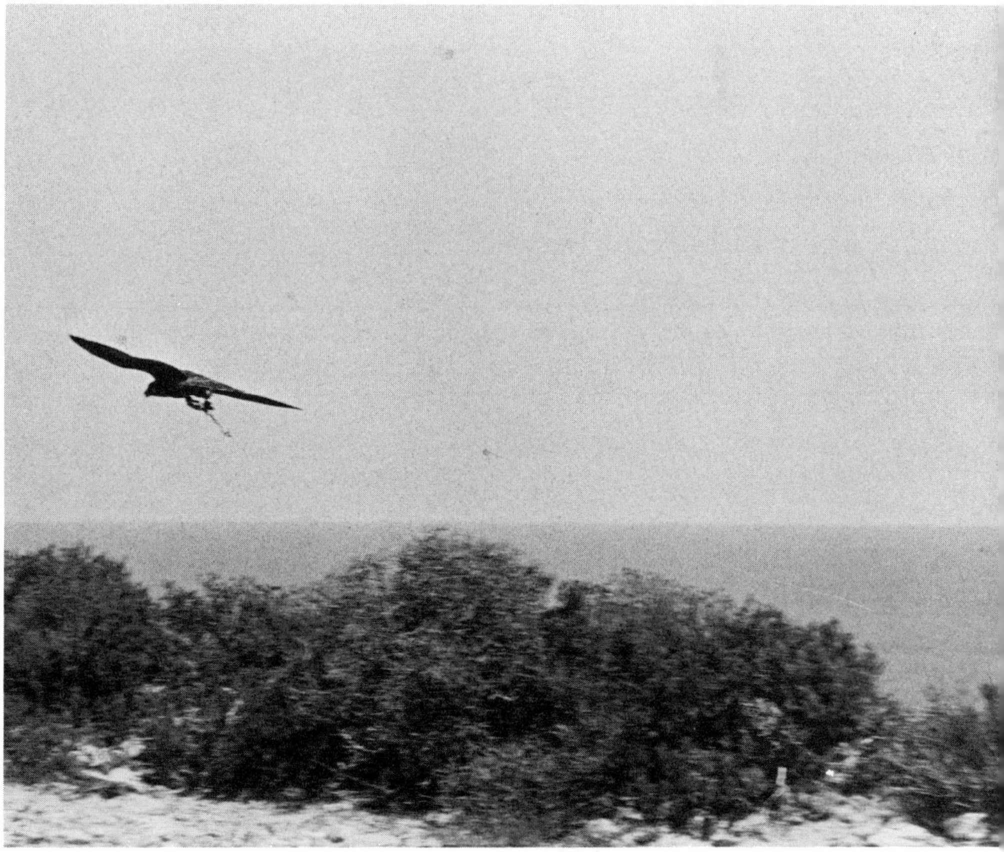

This is the halfway house, a crumbled bastion of some long-forgotten power. On one side it looks to the sea, on the other to the moor. When the bird returns, it waits here for the man.

. . . and the man just watches because he knows that wild open places make a call that must be answered.

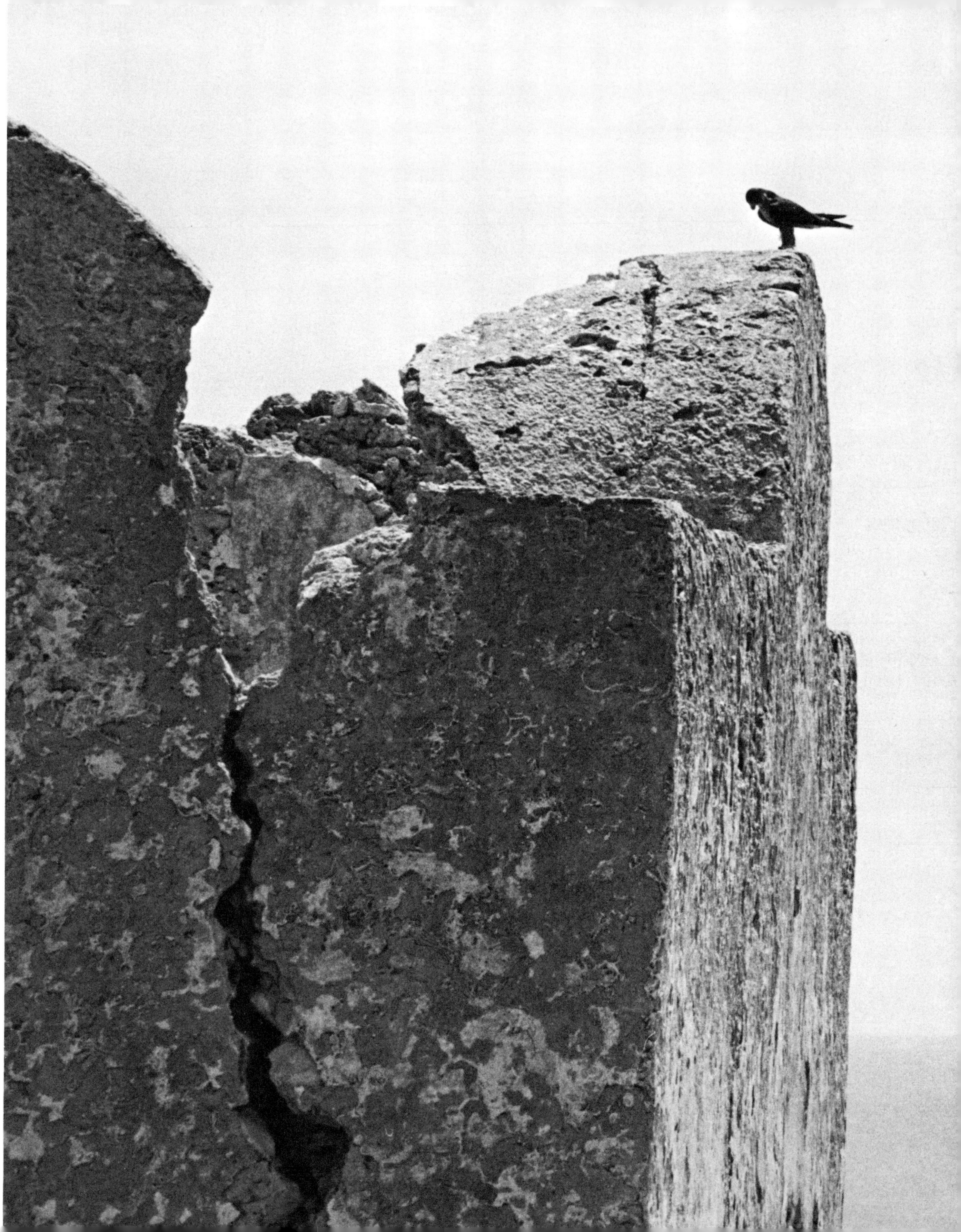

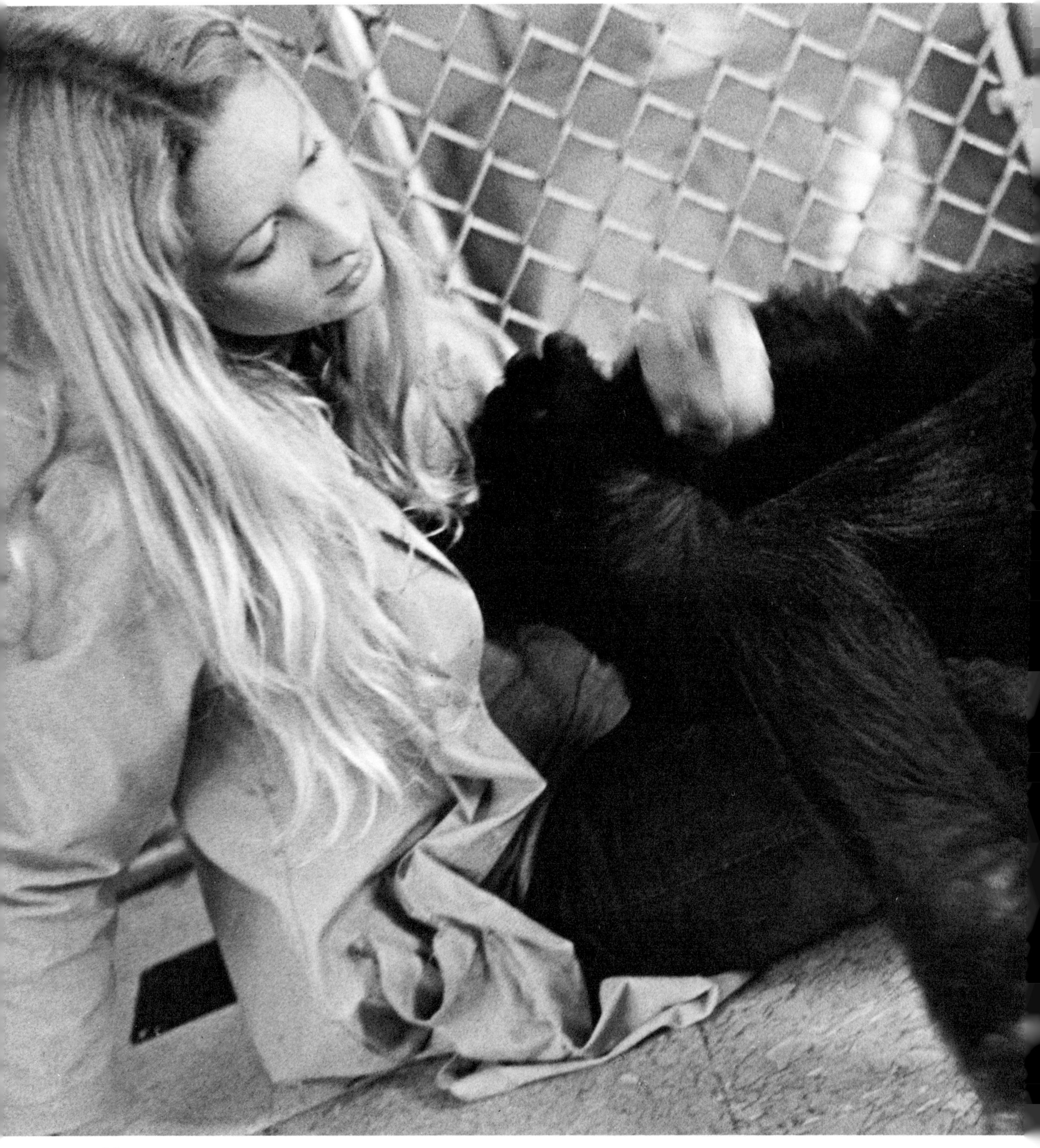

One Great Ape

No truth appears to me more evident than that the beasts are endowed with thought and reason as well as men. The arguments are in this case so obvious that they never escape the most stupid and ignorant.
—DAVID HUME:
  A Treatise of Human Nature, *IV, 1739*

She was a pale, sensitive, skinny kid with long legs and long blond hair that her mother called "stringy." She did all the things the other kids did. She did her homework and did well in school because she was bright and dutiful. She got along all right with everybody, had some pretty good friends, took lessons for a while in this and for a while in that. Her family thought she was shy, perhaps because she spent so much time alone in her room. But she wasn't shy. Penny was leading a double life.

Everybody thought Penny was a nice, ordinary, middle-class American kid. Everybody, that is, except Ugly the dog, Pretty the cat, and Pretty Ugly the hamster. They knew. They knew that Penny the schoolgirl was a beautifully contrived front for Mow-Gla the Jungle Girl, Queen of the Animals. For Penny and the animals understood each other. Penny was one of those rare kids born with the gift of speaking with animals. And all animals immediately recognized her as their queen.

So effective was Penny's ability to disguise her true identity that even when she went to the zoo to visit her subjects, the people just saw a quiet skinny little girl standing awkwardly and looking long at each animal. They couldn't see the tall, beautiful, passionate Mow-Gla, regal yet kind, favoring each of her subjects with just the right remark to give them the courage and patience they so badly needed.

Sometimes in her dreams Penny would let some favored human see her as she really was, and needless to say, they were thunderstruck. Often, when she was alone in her room, Penny would elaborate on these dreams and have fantastic imaginary adventures with her animal friends. But perhaps these weren't fantasies at all. . . .

I don't know if that's the way it really was, but I'll bet I'm not too far off base. For now, twenty years later, Penny Patterson is a psychologist—an animal psychologist. Her present life started over five years ago when she went with her Stanford University faculty adviser to the San Francisco Zoo to observe some gorillas and to see if some research arrangement could be worked out. Nothing evolved from that, but at about that time several events occurred: Penny heard the Gardners talk about their pioneering study of speech and language formation, using great apes in their laboratory; and she learned that the supposedly male gorilla at the San Francisco Zoo had just had a baby. The zoo was so excited by this unexpected windfall that they simply apologized for their mistake in sexing the gorilla and kept their gorilla family carefully intact. Well, captive gorillas don't always make good mothers (or maybe this one, having been brought up as a male, wasn't quite prepared), and the baby didn't do very well. It developed severe dysentery and malnutrition, so it had to be removed from its family to the zoo nursery. All this while Penny was excitedly and intensively studying American Sign Language (Ameslan), the standard language for the deaf, in hopes of using it in her work with animals.

Shortly after the gorilla baby was finally cured, at about nine months, Penny got permission to work with it at the zoo nursery. Her Stanford advisers accepted as a doctoral thesis her proposal to teach a gorilla to talk, and the director of the zoo agreed to lend her the gorilla. He also helped her find a trailer for the two of them to live in. That was about four years ago.

Koko is now five years old. She never fully recovered from her early illness and still has what delicate people call "a delicate stomach." She is a little clumsy with fine movements, and she's six months behind other five-year-olds—human ones, that is—in her re-

Koko complains a little, but you can see who's really hurting.

sponses to standard intelligence testing. Like other youngsters, Koko is generally affable, playful, a little high-strung (easily frightened by loud noises, for example), not especially affectionate in a physical way, but obviously attracted to petite women—and passionately dependent on and devoted to her "mother," Penny. Koko has been brought up in much the same way a dedicated middle-class mother might bring up a mute, hyperactive American child. She lives in a small trailer apartment (with a bedroom–living room–kitchen railroad-flat arrangement) and is never separated from her "mother" for long. She has almost as full a vocabulary and the toilet-training, eating, and play habits of any human five-year-old. She uses about three hundred word signs fluently, another two hundred equivocally, and can combine two, three, or four signs. She uses her potty without fail, assists in planning her meals, converses freely and initiates conversations (to make her feelings and thoughts clearly known), uses eating utensils properly (table manners vary in different homes)—and she's strong enough to kill a man.

After my visit with Koko (November 1976), I returned to my hotel and immediately made some notes on my tape recorder:

The trailer stands just behind the museum on the campus of Stanford University. I knocked on the door and Penny asked me to wait a minute. From the sounds, I gathered that she was putting Koko into her room. Then she let me in. I came into a narrow kitcheny kind of room with a sink, refrigerator, and some counter space. Koko was in the next room. The rooms were separated by heavy chain-link walls and doors. On a blackboard next to the entrance were written the "words of the month"—the words that Penny is trying to teach Koko during the course of the current month. I noticed about twenty words. One can count the exact number if the photograph is clear enough. The light was very low so I may have some difficulties. The door between Koko's central room and Penny's end room (kitchen and office) where I stood was closed. Koko came immediately to the door as I opened it and looked at me very curiously. Penny went to Koko and said, "Koko, here is a new friend. Would you like to meet him?" When Penny signs to Koko in Ameslan, she always automatically speaks the words out loud, and she does the same whenever Koko is signing. She does it so automatically that when Koko was talking to me later it seemed as if Penny were Koko's voice. In this instance Koko said, "Let me out!"

Penny opened the door and Koko came over to me, about two steps worth. She came very, very close, seized me on both upper arms, and put her face very close to mine. I held her sides and told her how nice she was and that I liked her and what a great-looking gorilla she was. While I was talking to her and flattering the hell out of her, she peered at me very intensely. With one of her hands she started to explore my face. Then she put her face very close to mine again and started to blow. Penny said that Koko wanted me to blow at her. I blew at her and we blew back and forth for a while from a distance of maybe a half-inch. Koko seemed satisfied, though I don't know whether it was because of her exploration of my face or my flattery or my blowing technique. She backed off a bit, took my hand in one of hers, and pulled me gently into her room. (I assume it was gentle, be-

127

cause I went along without reservation.) Once we got into the room she made some signs to me, and Penny said, "Tickle my foot!" I was momentarily taken aback, but I quickly oriented myself and reached down for Koko's foot to accommodate her, but she promptly scampered away. From across the room she made some signs and Penny (who seemed to be writing in a book and not paying much attention to us) said, "The game is to chase me and tickle my foot!" I proceeded to chase Koko. I could corner her fairly readily, either against a barrier or in a corner of the room, but then she would position herself in such a way that I couldn't reach her foot. And she kept wrapping herself around in various ways and grabbing me with various things so that when something stuck out or grabbed me I couldn't tell immediately if it was a hand or a foot. It got to be kind of a wrestling match —but "match" is the wrong word. Although it was obvious that Koko was being very gentle, she's so strong that I lost heart within a minute or so—to say nothing of my wind—and I withdrew. She wasn't having any of that. She came over, made those signs, and I tried it again. This went on for maybe five or ten minutes, at the end of which time I had really had it. I was thoroughly wiped out. I had a cut on one hand which Koko had grabbed a little too vigorously so that one of her nails dug in. When Penny saw this, she admonished Koko for playing too roughly, telling her to stop it and that there would be no more playing for a while and suggesting that she come and have breakfast.

Next came a long interchange during which Penny and Koko established the breakfast menu. Penny asked Koko, "What do you want?" Koko decided she wanted apple juice and a pear and a banana, I think it was. Penny kept up a constant running conversation with Koko about her behavior, her moods, her wishes—much as a doting mother would do with a young child. At the same time, Penny would make a note every time Koko used a word or an expression that she was trying to keep track of.

After breakfast, which was rather a drawn-out affair, Koko went to the potty in her room and urinated quite unself-conciously. She then came over to me for some more playing and some more tickling. This time she wanted to have her neck tickled. I had an easier time with that because she wasn't playing any wrestling games with me or running away too much. She was much more ticklish on her neck, and she enjoyed it so obviously, scrunching her head down on my tickling hand, that I liked doing it.

Then Koko decided she was hungry again, went to the refrigerator, opened the door, and took out a jar of baby-food pudding. Penny said she couldn't have it because it belonged to the younger gorilla (a recent acquisition) at the other end of the trailer. Koko was not impressed. She took the jar and insisted on having the custard. Like any indulgent mother, Penny didn't protest too much but went to look for a spoon. Koko took the spoon, unscrewed the cap from the jar, and declared herself "happy!" Then with great gusto she ate the pudding. She cleaned out the jar very skillfully with the spoon and finished up by sticking a long tongue into the jar and licking out whatever she had been unable to reach with the spoon. Then she played with the spoon and the empty jar for a while.

Penny offered Koko a variety of toys but she took little interest in them. Koko went to

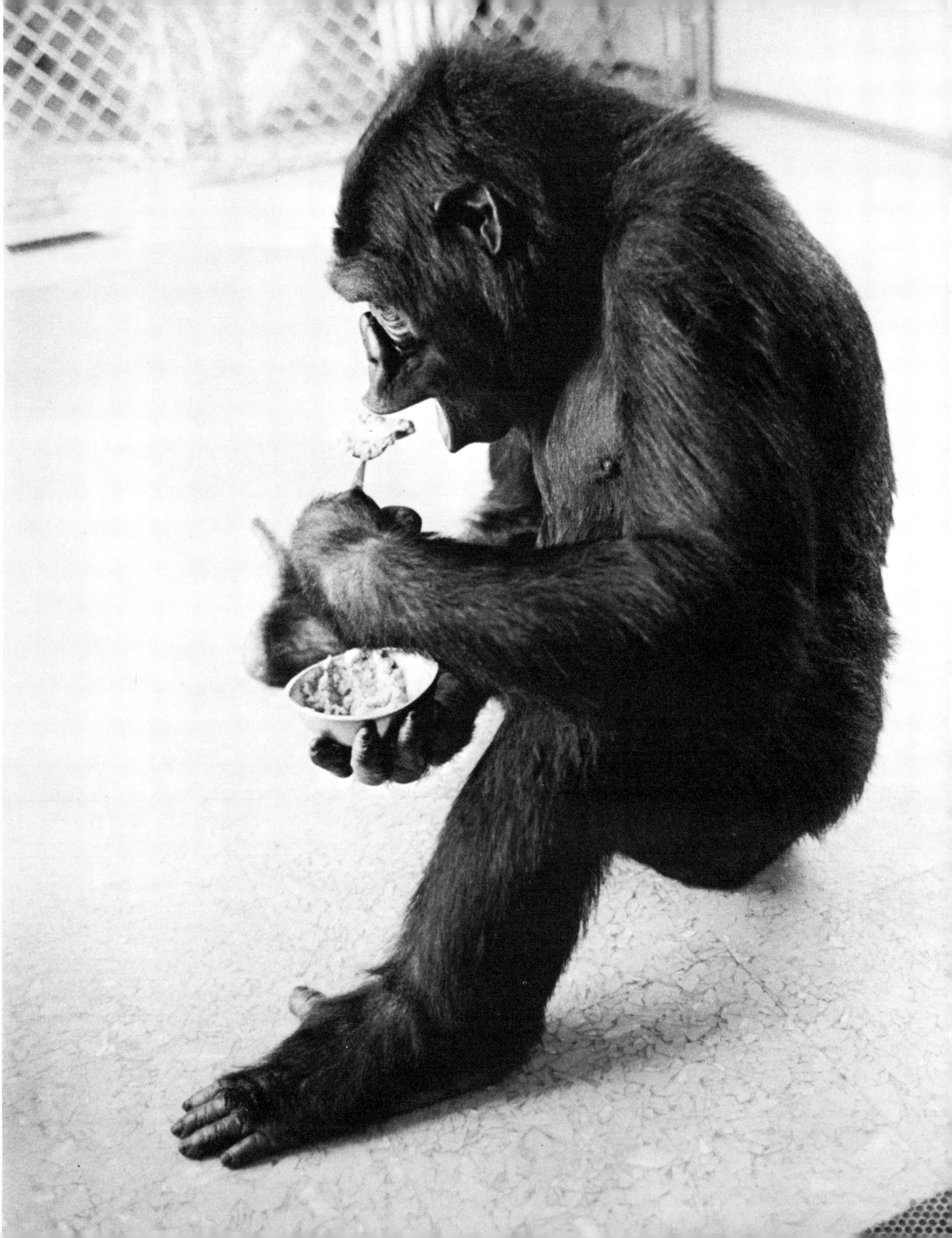

the closet, opened it, and pulled out a bunch of rags and cloth. Penny said, "Well, she's going to make a nest." Koko selected several of these rags (she was quite discriminating but I couldn't figure out what qualified a rag as prime nest material), pushed them around on the floor, lay down on them, promptly got up, took a large cloth, covered her face with it, announcing that it was "red." And so it was. Penny said that Koko associates "red" with "angry" and sometimes announces that she is "red mad," which reminded me of the expression "seeing red." This association didn't seem relevant at the time, however, because Koko proceeded to go through some of the other cloths, naming the colors. She got them all right and I thought Penny was proud.

Penny offered Koko a jigsaw puzzle, which she declined, and then a piece of paper, which she accepted. Koko announced her intention to draw and asked for a pencil, but when she got the pencil she just bit off the end. Penny scolded her and made her spit it out. Koko looked chastened (a little) and said she was "sorry for being bad." But she obviously had no real interest in drawing, so Penny got out a notebook with some pictures in it. She and Koko looked at the pictures, commenting to each other. Koko recognized pictures of a number of common objects and said "gorilla" when they came to what looked to me to be a pretty bad drawing of a gorilla's face.

Koko then found a thin rubber glove somewhere. Penny wanted to teach her the sign for "glove," but Koko was intent on getting Penny to put the glove on her (Koko's) hand. They discussed this a bit. Koko kept shoving her hand at Penny until the glove was about half on, and then she ran into her section of the trailer with it dangling from her hand. She played for a while with the glove and then, with a dreamy look in her eyes, she chewed it to pieces.

After this, Koko sidled over to me and suddenly, quick as a flash, she grabbed my tape recorder, ran into her room with it, and begin to punch the buttons. I let out a yell and Penny came and retrieved the tape recorder. She scolded Koko firmly, but I had the wild idea that she thought it was cute the way Koko was jabbing at the buttons.

Penny went back to her work and, as if determined to make me uncomfortable, Koko came back to me, pulled my sweater, reached underneath it, and started to tickle me. She wasn't a gentle tickler, and I didn't find it pleasant at all. In fact, I felt that she'd manhandled me long enough. Considering her strength, she had been very gentle and careful, but she was nevertheless tiring to play with, as any five-year-old would be. So when she pulled my sweater again and reached under to tickle me, I finally protested. Penny scolded her. Koko said, "Koko is a bad gorilla" and backed away. Now that we were all agreed I felt better.

Koko came over immediately, took my hand ever so gently, drew me to her, put her face very close to mine, and blew softly. We

blew at each other for a while, and that was fine. During this time she would take hold of me, feel me with her hands, and put her lips on my face. For a short period of time we both sat on the floor just holding hands.

Then Penny went out to help feed the younger gorilla, and I left too, to get some fresh air and to relax a little. I had been swarmed over by this gorilla for about two hours by that time.

When Penny returned, we entered the trailer again. Koko immediately asked to have the door opened so she could come into the office with us. Penny said, "No, I think not.

You were bad. You were a bad gorilla. You stole the tape recorder and tickled your new friend roughly, and that's bad." Koko said, "Koko sorry. Promise good. I promise to be good." Penny replied, "You're not sorry. You're just saying that because you want me to open the door." Koko kept repeating, "Koko is sorry. Koko promise good. Please open the door." But Penny was adamant. It turned out that she had to leave anyway. She said that she had a few chores to do. It was clearly time for me to go too.

On the way back to my hotel, the whole experience was muddling around in my mind —not so much what actually happened as what all of this means. It is undeniable that human beings and animals can talk to each other, and it is undeniable that Koko has a sophisticated range of intellectual and emotional responses. As I walked down the street thinking about this and trying to get my head together, I passed a large English sheep dog tied to a post. Our eyes met and I was jerked out of my reverie by the intensity of the dog's gaze. It's not an uncommon experience to catch a dog's eye as you pass him, and I always say "hello" when it happens to me. But this dog caught me at a moment when the barrier between species was fuzzy in my mind, and I had the distinct impression that he was saying something to me—something he was thinking or feeling, like: "Wow, where have you been? Where did you pick up that wild odor?" I don't know. It was a meaningful encounter. It moved me. It suddenly seems conceivable that one could teach a dog to talk. Or some other animal. Or all animals. And it's conceivable that their thoughts and feelings would surprise us.

That's the end of the notes I made when I got back to my room in San Francisco. Weeks have passed since then—event-filled, life-filled weeks—but this experience has been constantly on my mind. At this moment I am most strongly touched by Koko's feelings. She *wanted* things, and sometimes she wanted them badly. She *had* to have that intriguing tape recorder, that luscious custard, Penny's reassuring attention. I can identify with that. That's the way *I* feel. When that wanting got

This is how you say "glove."

"I'd rather do it than say it."

her into trouble, she was abashed and upset. That's the way it happens to me, too. And then I think about what will happen if the San Francisco Zoo takes her back (as they are trying to do), away from her home and her Penny. She'll feel the way I would feel—and I can't bear the thought.

I used to feel a little superior to those sentimental people who anthropomorphize animals. It used to make me faintly nauseated when some lady would tell me about her little dog, "Oh, poor dear Minette always feels so *left out* when I'm chatting with friends." But why do *you* think Koko clamored to be let into the office when Penny and I were talking there?

One incident in the trailer comes back to me now. We were all together in Koko's room, and Penny was trying to explain something to me. After a couple of minutes Koko came over, put her hand on my chest, and shoved me so that I staggered back a few steps.

135

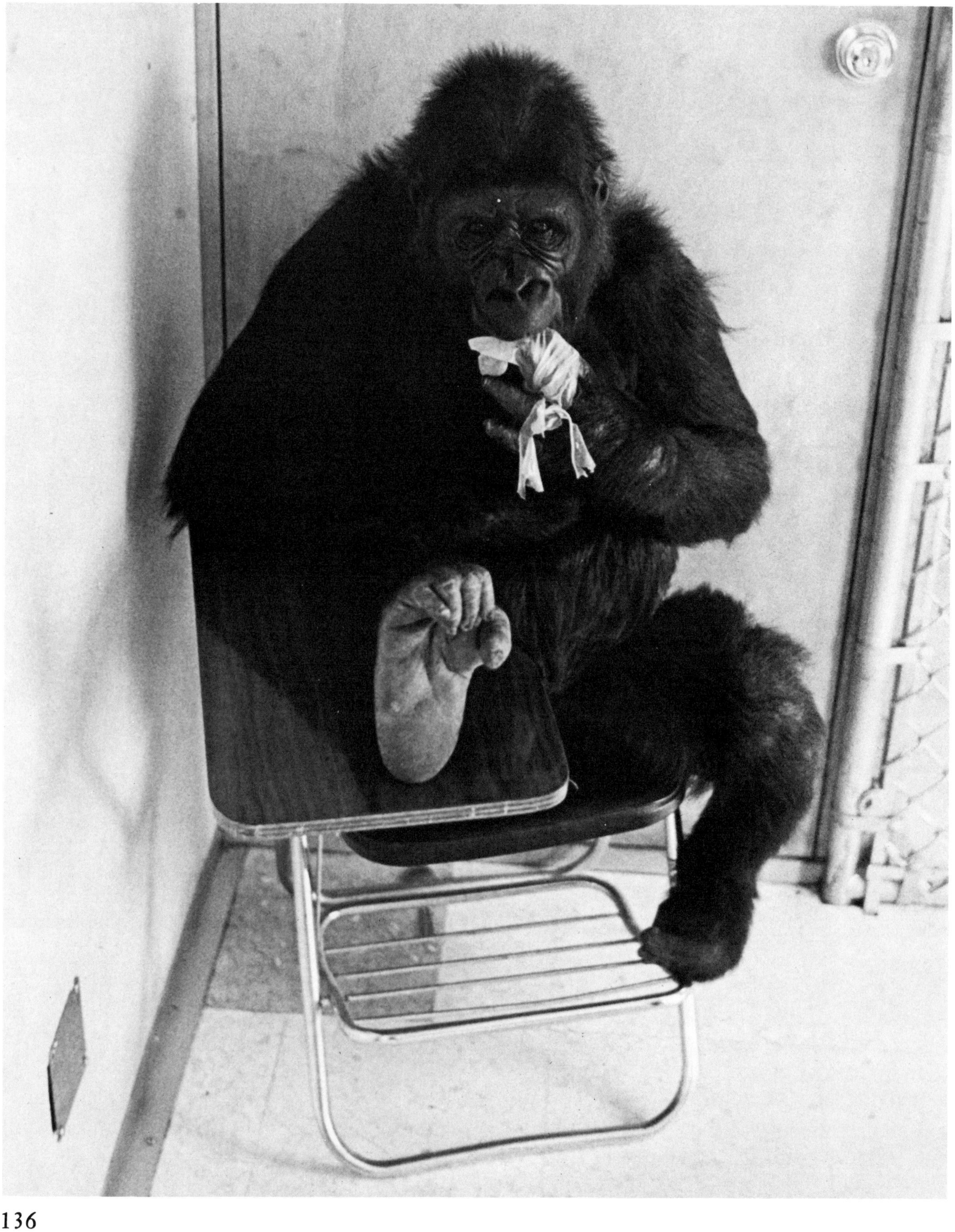

Penny gave her hell but I protested, "Oh, c'mon, let her be. She didn't mean anything. It's all right." I realize now that I took Koko's part because I knew how she felt. But so did Penny, judging from her reply: "Yes, she did mean something. That wasn't in fun. All this hassle with the zoo has been interfering with our relationship and she's been deprived."

Love, joy, sorrow, despair, guilt, rage, fear—that's the stuff of life. If I were to tell you about an incident that happened to me which you had experienced yourself, you might say, "Yeah, right on, man!" You would recognize and delight in our communion. Picture yourself responding that way to a gorilla, as I did. There is every reason to believe that if we took the trouble to teach all gorillas to talk, as we take the trouble to teach all human beings, we would respond that way to all gorillas: "Yeah, right on, gorilla!" Well, there aren't very many gorillas, and we could easily encompass their paltry number without even noticing it (although it might take some getting used to). Since Koko's intelligence-testing is within human range, since Penny's smaller gorilla shows even more promise than

"I'd sooner eat it than say it or do it."

Koko, and since it's fashionable to point out this sort of thing about minority groups, I might even suggest that they could make great contributions!

Of course, if such a trend were started, who knows where it might end? A lot of chimpanzees have been taught to "talk," and some great apes actually "talk" to each other in the words they have learned. I am convinced that other animals will eventually be similarly taught. Perhaps we will find that we share with them what used to be thought of as great, fundamental human experiences.

There are any number of scientific, philosophic, and logical reasons why animals supposedly can't learn to talk—some degree of crude communication, perhaps, but "talk," no. We'll have to push that back a little now and admit that primates can be taught to talk a little. But "lower" animals? No way, the experts say. My personal guess is that the logic for this stand is impeccable but that its foundation is shaky. I have confidence that scientists will be dogmatically skeptical and then will go at it and disprove their own skepticism. It's always been that way. So I say animals can be taught to talk and I say it's not going to stop with primates.

One of Buddha's qualities has been described like this: "He dwells compassionate and kind to all creatures that have life." I don't think this attitude was a moral one. I just think Buddha *knew*. I think if you know *enough*, it comes out right. And there are different kinds of "knowing" and different ways of achieving it. I "know" a great deal more as a result of my experience with Koko. Most of it cannot be expressed, but it's there all right.

It's funny how people react when I tell them about Koko. For each one it raises questions, and of course the questions are different because they reflect personal preoccupations. My own obsession is about barriers, about walls between people, between groups, between people and animals, between anything. My obsession has to do with being closed and alone instead of "knowing" enough to be open. So I asked myself a particular set of questions, the ones expressed in this book. Some people have said to me, "Gee, Koko sounds so human! I wonder if she has a soul?" I can't deal with that kind of question. For that the answer will have to come from a higher authority. I can't answer the questions that this story brings up in your mind. You will have to do that yourself. I hope you try.

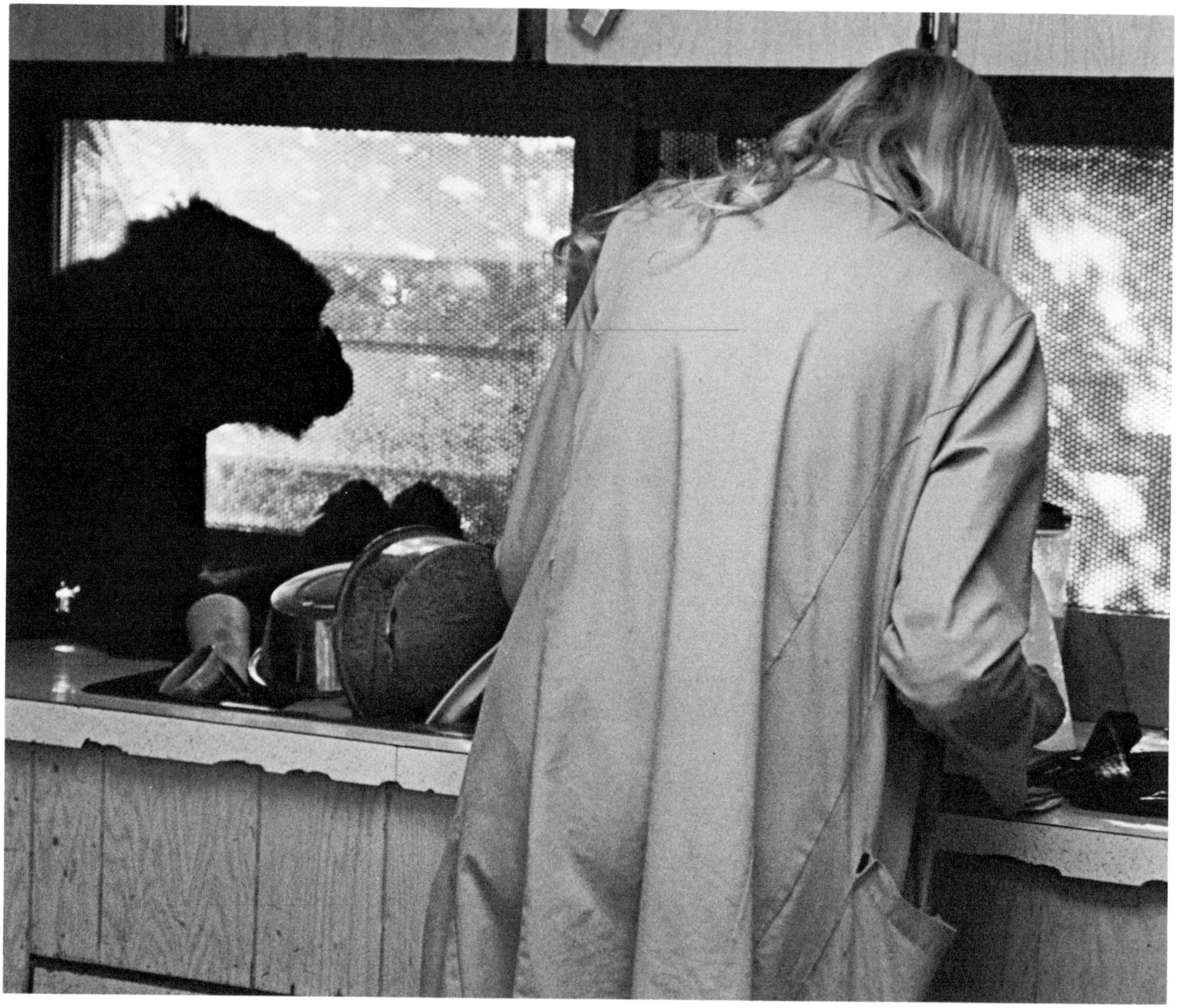

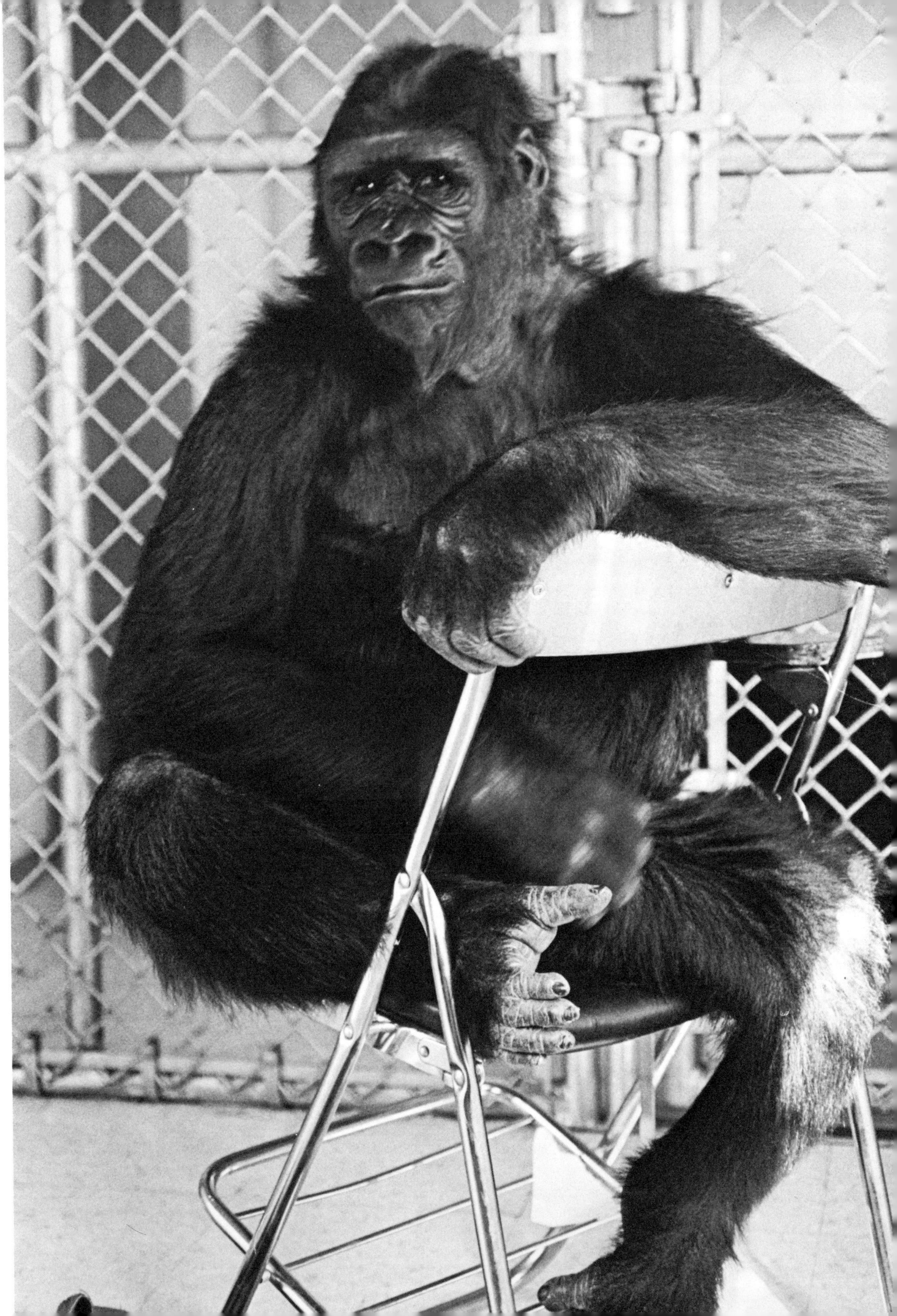

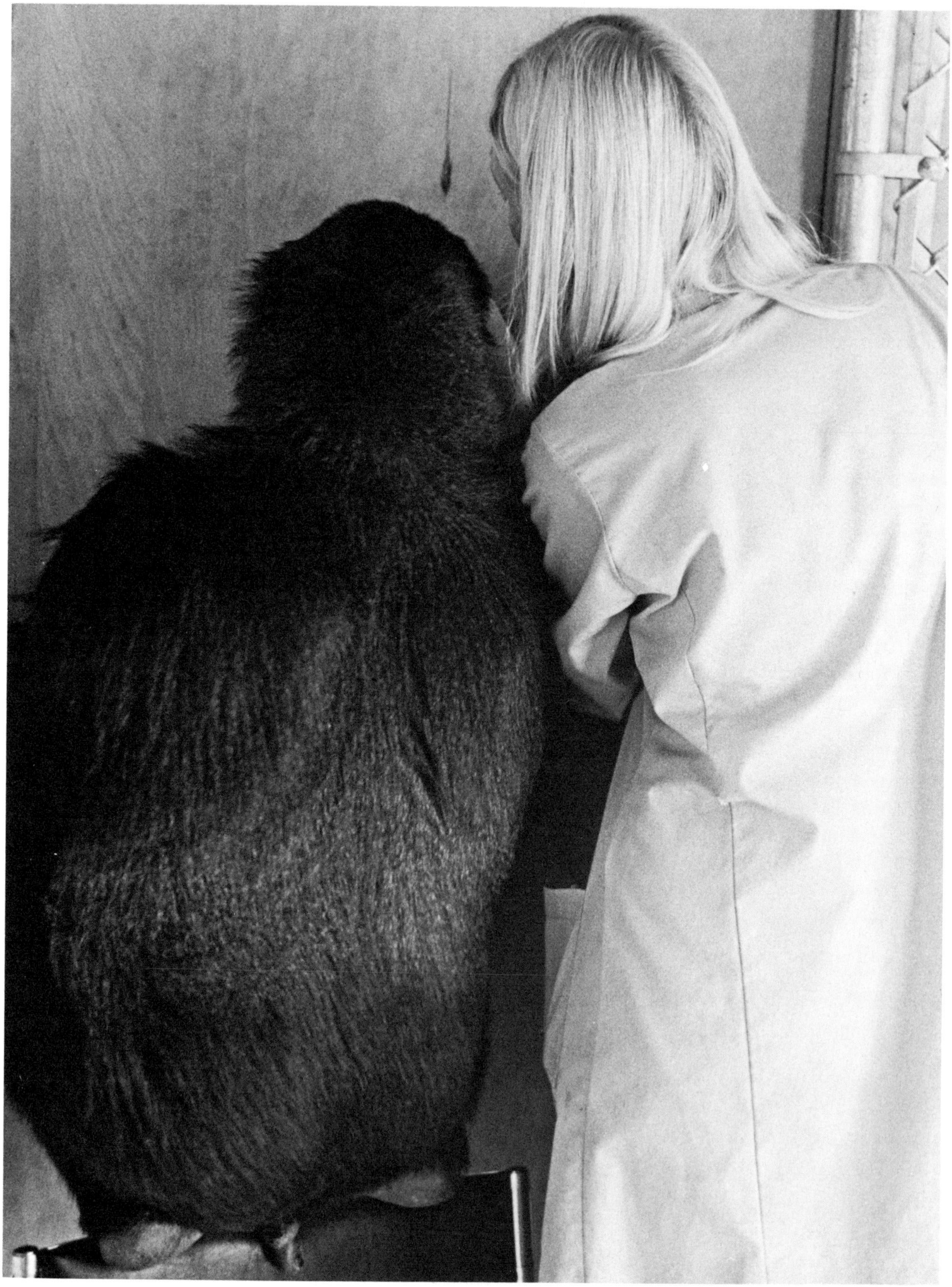

Afterword

There are some things I'd like you to know about that didn't seem to fit anywhere in the book. All the people mentioned in the book received me openly, freely, and graciously. They were all ready, willing, and able to be honestly giving of themselves. They are all outstanding human beings. I feel the greatest respect and gratitude in each instance.

Every book has an editor. In addition to being a sort of liturgist in the Temple of Publishing, a repository of any kind of information one might need, an arbiter of literary taste, and a subtle smoother of frayed emotions—in additon to all that, my editor is the nicest person. And she's pretty, too. Her name is Barbara Burn.

I'm not being self-indulgent in telling you how my family suffered. One of my children is going to be a writer like his Daddy: he's going to write a book called *Life without Father*. They not only missed me, they missed me most when I was there. If a book is messing around inside you, you just can't turn it off at five or six o'clock in the evening—or any other appropriate time. So Gretchen, my wife, had to read all kinds of drafts and look at all kinds of pictures. She's the busiest person I know, yet she read and looked with an objectivity and clarity of perspective that kept me from foundering in a sea of enthusiastic narcissism.

A few matters concerning Koko should be clarified. Penny originally acquired Koko on a loan from the San Francisco Zoo. It was understood that the loan was to be renewable. Since that time the director, with whom she had an oral understanding, left. It's now several directors later, the original understanding has become somewhat obscured, and the present administration of the zoo wants Koko back for breeding. Since the issue is so highly charged emotionally, it should in all fairness be pointed out that the San Francisco Zoo is not being mean or arbitrary. The zoo is trying to carry out its responsibility. It feels that the longer Koko remains with Penny, the less chance she'll have to adapt well to her ultimate life in the zoo (which is, after all, her legal residence). They may also be concerned that unless they get Koko soon, even if she adapts to zoo life, she may never be relaxed enough there to breed. Zoos must be very concerned with breeding, especially of those species whose numbers in the wild are limited. Of course, Penny has a good answer for each of these considerations, but I want to point out that the zoo does have issues to be considered.

At one point the San Francisco Zoo agreed to accept a substitute gorilla if Penny could supply one, but, to put it bluntly, Penny just doesn't have the money to go out and buy a gorilla. She also needs more gorillas for her own project, as well as equipment and personnel to work with. In an attempt to meet these needs a tax-deductible foundation has been formed: The Gorilla Foundation at P. O. Box 3002, Stanford, California 94305.

For the sake of accuracy I want to clarify that, though I reported Koko's conversations as Penny translated them to me, in a subsequent communication Penny told me that the translations are not literal since Ameslan does not have a symbol for every word in English.

For example, Koko might make two signs, "Koko" and "gorilla," and Penny would translate that, "I am a gorilla."

You should know that I'm uneasy about the falcon story. Something in that episode touched off in me a strong negative emotional response. During the experience itself I tried not to let my discomfort intrude, although I did ask Heinz Meng why he had given that lady such a hard time. Only in the course of writing the chapter did the nature and strength of my feeling become really clear. I have to leave the chapter as it is because that's the way it was. On the other hand, it's pretty poor repayment for Heinz's kind and helpful attitude. I don't know what I can do other than to write what I have to write and to say that I'm sorry—which I am.

Together with John Kaufmann, Heinz Meng has written a book called *Falcon's Return* about how the peregrine has been bred in captivity in an attempt to resue an endangered species. At least equally interesting to me, however, are the wonderful descriptions of falcons in the wild and of the practice of falconry.

By the time you read this, Danny will probably be in Indonesia teaching his methods to elephant trainers there. It won't be his first foreign venture, since, at the request of the People's Republic of China, he spent some time as a guest in Peking instituting an elephant-training school.

Sad to report, as of this moment the New York City Police Department Mounted Unit training program has fallen victim to that city's financial woes. Since, however, both financial and political matters are notoriously subject to ups and downs, we are awaiting the return of good times patiently and confidently.

Again by the time you read this, I am confident that Captain Haggerty will have expanded.

I heard a rumor that Norman has been elected to the vestry of the Church of the Holy Trinity.

Arnie is staying with the dolphin team only because he feels that Jim needs him. He thinks he really belongs with the killer whales.

I went to the Bronx Zoo the other day. There's a very placid and amiable camel that gives children rides. He spat at me.